Nanny Goat Island
Dungeness Then and Now

Also by Keith Swallow

The Book of Syn:
Russell Thorndike, Dr Syn and the Romney Marsh

Much Drinking in the Marsh
A History of the Pubs and Breweries of Romney Marsh

Despite being born and raised in Surrey, Keith Swallow has had a lifelong obsession with both the coast and Romney Marsh, and moved to East Sussex in 1993 to be nearer to the sea. Having taken early retirement from a career in auditing, he now has more time to indulge his hobbies of local history, sport and sea kayaking – when not propping up the bars of local public houses. He is married with two grown-up children.

Nanny Goat Island

Dungeness Then and Now

Keith Swallow

Edgerton Publishing Services
Pett, East Sussex

First published in Great Britain in 2019 by
Edgerton Publishing Services
Jasmine Cottage, Elm Lane, Pett, Hastings, East Sussex TN35 4JD
Tel. +44 (0) 1424 813003
Email enquiries@eps-edge.co.uk

Reprinted with minor changes in 2021

Copyright © 2019 by Keith Swallow

Keith Swallow has asserted his rights under the Copyright Designs and Patents Act, 1988 to be identified as the author of this work.

All rights reserved. No part of this publication may be reproduced, stored in a retrieval system, or transmitted, in any form or by any means, electronic, mechanical, photocopying, recording, or otherwise without written permission.

The book is sold subject to the condition that it shall not by way of trade or otherwise, be lent, resold, hired out, or otherwise circulated without the publisher's prior consent in any form of binding or cover other than that in which it is published and without a similar condition being imposed on the subsequent purchaser.

ISBN: 978-0-9933203-4-7

A CIP catalogue record for this book is available from the British Library.

Typeset in Garamond by Edgerton Publishing Services.

Printed and bound in Great Britain by Ashford Colour Press, Gosport, UK

Every effort has been made to trace and acknowledge ownership of copyright of the illustrations used in this book. The publisher will be pleased to make suitable arrangements to clear permission with any copyright holders whom it has not been possible to contact.

Dungeness — 1887

A vast expanse of wild and barren strand,
But sparsely clothed with verduand with flowers
In sweet confusion mingled: while there towers
High over all the Light-house. Close at hand
In mighty force the storms rage, as I stand
To watch the vessels scud before the gale;
And hear, of wrecks the horror-laden tale
That thrilled impulsive hearts throughout the land.
No spot, than this, more desolate remains,
Yet with the place, my fondest wishes dwell,
For deeds of manly daring fling strong chains
Of memory around it: I could tell
Of honest Truth and Love, with fewest pains
All linked to Dungeness – Heaven bless it well!

Joseph Castle ("Curate to the Coast")

Dungeness — 1996

There's still a vast expanse of barren strand
But less than formerly, for towering there
The great Power Station buildings, bleak and bare
Even eclipse the lighthouse, though two stand –
One working, and one just a tourist trap
Where all who have the energy may toil
Up winding stairs to view the stony soil
Still ridged and flower-decked in nature's lap.
Here, as in Castle's day, the Lifeboat men
Ready and willing, brave the stormy seas
But rather than the Coastguards who were then
The main inhabitants, the dwellings please
Holidaymakers, bird-life watchers, when
They watch for rarities upon the breeze.

Margaret Bird (Romney Marsh historian)

It is not a picturesque landscape, it is an atmosphere, a large flat area illuminated
like no other place in England, where the sea is supreme.
Brian Yale: *Dungeness – Landscapes on the Edge*

If Kent is the Garden of England, Dungeness is the back gate"
New York Times

Contents

Author's Preface viii

Acknowledgements and Disclaimer xi

1. Overview: The (Un)Natural landscape and its Colonisation 1
2. Fishing – a Way of Life 17
3. Defence of the Realm – Wartime 37
4. War on Smuggling – Revenue Protection 59
5. Saving the Mariner – Coastguard and Lifeboat Services 65
6. Serving the Mariner – Aids to Navigation and Shipping 81
7. Cometh the Railways – Plans for Development;
   Rail & Other Transport Links 103
8. Going Nuclear – The Dungeness Power Stations 127
9. For the Birds (and Other Species) – A Special Place for Nature 137
10. Serving the Public – Amenities and Services 147
11. Ownership, Tourism and Management 169
12. A Final Mystery 189

Appendices
   A. Detailed Timeline 191
   B. Bibliography 199
   C. Dungeness in Film and Other Media 201

Author's Preface

When I set out to write an account of the development of this part of the coast, it encompassed Littlestone, Greatstone, Lade and Lydd-on-Sea, in addition to Dungeness. It soon became clear, however, that the rich history of Dungeness demanded its own separate narrative.

Dungeness has now become a most unlikely tourist attraction, drawing up to a million visitors each year. First experiences are pivotal – whether it be on a tranquil summer's day with a heat haze shimmering over the shingle; or in bleak midwinter, when the wind can howl so mercilessly that you yearn to get straight back into the car. It is the largest expanse of shingle in Europe, and only South America can boast a larger feature of this type. Incredibly, it contains 600 species of plants (a third of all those to be found in the UK), and has birdlife in abundance.

Those who live on the 'Ness have for long ploughed their own furrow. Life here has rarely been easy and, for many years, the provision of even basic creature comforts was dependent on sea conditions and the vagaries of the fishing fields. Yet those who were born and raised here invariably speak fondly of magical, albeit simple, childhoods, where restrictions were few and nature was always to the fore. Although the unrealised plans to build a huge ferry terminal resulted in one of the most under-utilised railway lines in the country, the lack of suitable transport links meant that, for many years, 'Nessers remained self-sufficient and kept goats to meet their needs for milk. As a result, other communities (particularly residents of nearby Lydd) referred to them as "nanny-goat islanders".

What constitutes Dungeness? In addition to the estate, for the purpose of this narrative I have included the area west of the Point to Pen Bars, bounded by an arbitrary line running due north back to the Lydd Road. This encompasses both the power station and the RSPB reserve. I have, in addition, included the strip of land either side of Battery Road. Whilst sitting just outside the Dungeness estate, this small area has nevertheless played an important role in the development of the village, accommodating strategic defensive facilities as well as a number of pivotal fishing families and related support services.

And what of the future? Dungeness has begun to change radically and – almost certainly – irretrievably, with very few of the original families now remaining and with the 1920s railway carriages gradually being turned into state-of-the art buildings, which are pushing prices beyond the reach of locals. Many properties are empty for much of the year and, for those individuals requiring paid employment, fishing, lighthouse keeping and coastguard roles are no longer the staple. Indeed, recent census data has shown residents involved more in care-home and service work. But by far the largest employer in the area is now the power station, the future of which has been the source of constant speculation. The same is also true of another significant local employer – Lydd Airport. With the pressure on all of the south east's airports, this has come under close scrutiny, with potential benefits to the local economy and employment opportunities having to be weighed against the environmental cost of any expansion. A rather alarming – and alarmist – view of what could happen here was provided by press reports in 1968. At that time, a completely new facility for a third London airport at Dungeness (rather than simply expansion of Lydd) was being discussed. It was envisaged that 450 houses in Dungeness and Greatstone would have had to be demolished to achieve this and that the population of the area would increase by a figure in the region of 50,000. Under these proposals, Greatstone would have become the new southern terminus of the Romney, Hythe & Dymchurch Railway!

The changing face of Dungeness: for many years up until 1957, the old Pilot Inn dominated the entrance to the estate (top, Chris Shore collection); and the same view in 2017 (below)

Nanny Goat Island

The other main threat to the area is that posed by extensive gravel extraction. Construction companies have tapped into the vast resources in the area and numerous pits have already been worked. There has been constant debate between conservationists and builders as to the risk that this presents. Whilst there is no doubt that the pits provide a very attractive habitat for a wide range of bird and other wildlife, the down side is not limited to the inevitable noise and inconvenience generated by the extra lorry traffic. Some locals fear that continued extraction could result in subsidence or even destabilisation of the whole coastal strip, leaving it more prone to coastal flooding. These fears were to an extent assuaged when, in 2014, Kent County Council agreed to allow a 12-year project to further exploit existing pits at Dungeness rather than authorise new extractions. Nevertheless, fishermen at Dungeness have expressed their concerns that this still presents a threat to safety, as well as upsetting the balance of nature.

Acknowledgements and Disclaimer

Although many books have been published about Romney Marsh, these have not, to date, included a discrete detailed history of Dungeness.

Outside of the reclamation of the area, some of the "facts" that have been more generally reported are contradictory, and many issues have remained unexplored. In particular, there is mystery and confusion surrounding the roles and locations of the signal stations, the "skipways" used by Dungeness fishermen to transport their catches, the operating dates of coastguard lookout stations at various points along the coast, and the exact role and longevity of the Dungeness stone crushing plant. And during the war, of course, the sensitivity and strategic importance of this part of the coast resulted in great secrecy, with attendant reporting restrictions. In addition, phrases in common usage (such as signal station, lookout, coastguard, Admiralty) have not always reflected official terminology. Research has been further hampered by some surprising gaps in local records, as well as a lack of formality. Houses, for example, have always had names – which have in some cases changed frequently – rather than numbers and retail ventures have often been *ad hoc*, short-lived and unrecorded. Because of this, family histories and the recollections of older members of the community are invaluable, and I have tried to gather and collate as many of these as possible.

By the same token, that a small number of individual families have so influenced development of the area poses its own problems in terms of interpreting events. Whilst family histories contain important information, there is always the risk that they have been presented in such a way as to paint relatives in the best possible light. Where family members have also held (relatively) high political office, objectivity is likely to be further compromised. Furthermore, in times when the media was more in awe of the rich and powerful, such figures could – and often did – manipulate what appeared in print. I have tried to be objective in my reading of such accounts, but acknowledge that some may view actions and incidents differently. Where there is ambiguity or lack of clarity, I have tried to take a pragmatic view as to the most likely scenario, but have also outlined possible alternatives. There are omissions and there will be errors: I apologise for these, but the intention is to record as much as possible for future generations, before it is lost forever.

Historic photographs have been assembled from numerous sources, although the majority have come from my own family collection and those of Ted Carpenter and Chris Shore. Others have been kindly provided by Terry Tracey, Mike Golding, Linda Stanton, David Read,

John Wimble and Steve Tart. Additional sources of photographs have included the Internet, booklets and postcards. In a few cases, I have established that companies which previously held copyright have gone out of business, with no indication as to whether rights were transferred to others. Some other photographs have previously appeared several times in numerous publications, with few clues to their origin or copyright status. I have tried to locate copyright holders, but this has not proved possible in all cases. A number of photographs originally appeared in two booklets written by local fisherman Ken Oiller: *Tales of an Ordinary Dungeness Man* and *Dungeness Remembered*. These were themselves taken from different collections and, whilst I believe that I have the necessary permission in each case to use them, there may be the odd exception. Furthermore, in some cases local people have allowed me access to their photographic collections, but are unsure of the origin of individual pictures (and some appear within several different family collections). Whilst individuals have given me their own permission to use pictures, if there has been an unwitting breach of copyright, that is down to me. If I have misrepresented ownership of any photographs, I apologise unreservedly; the publisher will be pleased to make suitable arrangements to clear permissions with copyright holders in such cases.

It is not possible to produce a book such as this without drawing on copious sources and the help of many. With this in mind, I am particularly grateful to the following: Owen Leyshon of the Romney Marsh Countryside Partnership and EDF (amongst the many hats that he wears); Chris Shore, the photographer who runs a studio out of Caithness at Dungeness; Linda Stanton for tireless research and introductions; Paul Copson, whose forefathers were so instrumental in the development of the Dungeness we know today; David Read for his input on the Dengemarsh outfall; Mike Trevett for his knowledge of Dungeness skipways; Colin Clayton for background detail on several WWII air crashes; Judith Richardson, Pat Richardson; Steve and Maria Tart; Mike Golding ("Dungie Mike"); Alison Noyes of The Watch House; Stephanie Ingham of Stonihoe Cottage; Paul Gibbs of Holiday Cottages; Jerry Warne of Birdline South East; Peter and Janet Thomas; and the excellent Lydd Museum and New Romney History Society, which have both been a valuable source of information. Finally, and not for the first time, I am indebted to that doyen of Romney Marsh history, Ted Carpenter, for his assistance and patience.

Keith Swallow
November 2019

1

Overview – The (Un)Natural Landscape and Its Colonisation

Development

The name Dungeness refers simply to a cape or headland at the edge of Denge Marsh, and Dungeness is in many ways a classic example of a cuspate (essentially triangular) foreland. Its development is an integral part of the reclamation of Romney Marsh, a story that has been told many times – and by those much more qualified to explain the physical processes. This is not the place to re-tell it in full, but an understanding is required to appreciate why Dungeness is such a unique place.

Some 90 million years or so before now, Southern England was covered by chalk. During the more recent ice ages of 2–3 million years ago, the majority of this chalk weathered away leaving the harder flint to be washed down to the floor of the English Channel. As the ice

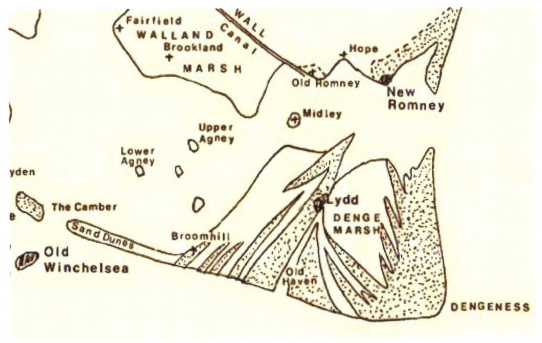

The build-up of shingle ridges that resulted in the formation of Dungeness (copyright status unknown)

melted, the sea level rose and over time the flint was carried eastwards along the Channel until it eventually started to pile up, ridge by ridge, at Dungeness. The shingle beach now exhibits some 600 ridges, which have developed over the last 5000–6000 years.

By the 16th century, Dungeness was starting to resemble something that we would recognise now. The Kent historian William Lambarde described it as follows: "the Neshe, called in Saxon Nesse . . . signifieth a Nebbe or Nose of the land extended into the sea". Similarly, the polymath William Camden recorded that: ". . . in the very utmost point of this Promontory, which the people call Dunge-nesse . . . there is nothing but beach and pible stones".

By the mid-19th century, Dungeness was widely referred to as "Adams" within reports and contemporary diary entries. Many coastal settlements at this time were known to fishermen by the nearest fishing station, although it is likely that, in this case, the name was taken from the family of Edward Adams. He and his ancestors were lighthouse keepers, at a time before dedicated accommodation was provided on site; accordingly, they probably lived in a cottage on the beach which would have been well-known to fishermen.[1]

Today, Dungeness is the largest expanse of shingle in Europe and, in world terms, second in size only to Patagonia.[2] It measures 12 km by 6 km (an area of 72 square kilometres), and in places is 17 m deep. It is comprised almost entirely of rounded pebbles, which range in size from pea gravel to medium cobbles, and these are 98% flint (the remainder being quartzite and sandstone). The expansion process may have slowed, but nevertheless continues today. The phenomenon of longshore drift particularly affects this part of the coast, with the natural wave action taking the shingle from west to east. The quantities involved are vast, with some 100,000 cubic metres being moved each year, mostly during the winter months. This means that the Ness continues to grow on its eastern side, at the expense of the southern/western shore, although the impact is mitigated to a large extent by the intervention of man. The building of the first nuclear power station on the Point in 1965 (and, subsequently, the current station in 1983) has meant that the stabilisation of Dungeness beach has become a priority, and this movement of shingle cannot be allowed to remain unchecked. Accordingly, to preclude the power stations being undermined, a convoy of lorries is employed to transport shingle back from whence it came. It is an unending process, but one that underlines the point that man cannot fully control nature.

It is the process by which Dungeness has developed that has also allowed the reclamation of what we now know as Romney Marsh, in its generic sense.[3] In pre-Roman times, the sea lapped the now inland cliffs between Rye and Hythe, but the accumulation of shingle at

---

1. Edward Adams died in 1833, at the age of 57. It was not until 1890 that the round base providing discrete keeper accommodation was added to the third lighthouse (see Chapter 6).
2. This seems to be the view of most geographers – although some claim that Florida's Cape Canaveral is the world leader. Measuring shingle is apparently not an exact science!
3. More properly, Romney Marsh comprises only a small area of land between New Romney and Hythe. Typically, however, the term is used to describe a much larger area, which also incorporates Walland Marsh, Denge Marsh and the Guldeford Levels.

1. Overview – The (Un)Natural Landscape & Its Colonisation

The development of the shingle ridges can clearly be seen when viewed from above – as from the old lighthouse (2017)

Dungeness first formed a bar or spit, which subsequently allowed man to recover land from the sea, parcel by parcel. The irony is that, whilst the reclaimed land was highly fertile and provided economic opportunities in terms of farming and salt mining, Dungeness – constantly exposed to salt-laden winds and with no naturally-occurring soil – was largely infertile.

The dynamic nature of the ongoing battle between land and sea throws up some interesting new features from time to time. One such arose as recently as 2016 when a storm, combined with the regular action of longshore drift, resulted in the creation of a huge lagoon within the shingle. This was in the vicinity of the lifeboat house and, as the picture below demonstrates, was large enough to comfortably accommodate a fishing boat. Although much

The 2016 "lagoon", created close to the lifeboat station (photo courtesy Linda Stanton)

of this was naturally infilled in the subsequent period, it was still quite discernible fully two years later.

Climate

Despite the urban myth, Dungeness is not, nor ever has been, a desert. Although climatic conditions do provide some challenges, its average annual rainfall of 700 mm is only a little below the UK average of 925 mm – and far above the general desert definition of 250 mm. It also falls well short of the day- and night-time temperature variation that characterises deserts. It is a mystery why the Met. Office is frequently incorrectly quoted as stating otherwise.

Long-standing residents advise that the seasons here are now less defined than they once were, which *is* confirmed by Met. Office data. Whilst this pretty much reflects a national trend, Dungeness winters in the mid-20th century were particularly harsh. The lakes would regularly freeze to a depth of up to a foot, and skating on the small lakes within the Ballast Hole area was a regular activity in the 1920s. In one particularly harsh winter, when gravel extraction was delayed for weeks, an (unsuccessful) attempt was made to free the dredging barges by placing explosives under the ice. Similarly, although there are occasions when some might dispute this(!), winds are rarely as fierce now as they were in the first half of the 20th century.

On a related issue, records maintained by local fishermen show that tide levels have been rising in recent years. Whether there is a direct link to climate change and/or global warming is a moot point, but high tides now quite regularly exceed eight metres; even 20 years ago such a state was almost unheard of.

Just occasionally, climatic conditions provide the visibility that allows distant views of the French coast (as pictured here in December 2017)

Water

The water table has a significant bearing on flora and fauna, but has been lowered over the last 50 years or so, owing not only to gravel extraction, but also to greater pumping activity to feed the local water supply. Increasingly, though, the construction and aggregate companies have engaged more positively with the Royal Society for the Protection of Birds (RSPB) and other organisations to mitigate damage to the environment and habitats. But open water at Dungeness is not solely the result of gravel extraction: a small proportion is naturally occurring – notably that in what are known as the Oppen Pits[4] on the RSPB Reserve. In the 13th century, these comprised two large and three smaller lagoons, which would have been saline; but, as the headland continued to grow, rainwater and percolation meant that they changed from salt to fresh water – with ecological impact. They are believed to now be the only wholly natural freshwater lakes remaining in south-east England. Old maps also show a number of other lakes at various times, the most significant being Wickmaryholm Pit. This migrated towards the shore, showing in the 19th century as a sizeable lake to the south of the current Lydd ranges – although it is arguably only on the edge of the area covered by this narrative. More firmly within the accepted borders of Dungeness was the Abnor Pit, to its east. Probably dating from Anglo-Saxon times, this became progressively infilled with shingle, although, as recently as the 1980s, it was still substantial enough to provide a reasonable walk around it. By 2015, it had all but disappeared – showing as little more than a small puddle.

Drainage

Being part of the wider Romney Marsh, Dungeness has an important role to play in its environmental management plans. Key to the survival of the Marsh, its inhabitants and economic well-being are the sea wall and an effective drainage system to ensure that the area is not reclaimed by the sea. There are two major components to the latter: the Royal Military Canal, which forms the northern boundary of Romney Marsh, and the network of ditches or "sewers" that provides a link between this and the sea. There are eight outfalls (or "guts") on the Marsh, with that at Dungeness (formally known as the Dengemarsh outfall) draining the western area of the Marsh. It is flanked by others at Littlestone to the north and The Brooks[5] to the west.

Because of the rough seas that characterise this part of the coast, there is a real danger of flooding in the event of a surge tide, and this risk is addressed in part by the implementation of a tidal flap at the point of entry of the Dengemarsh outfall (at Pen Bars) to the sea. The first flapped tidal outfall was installed in 1937, probably by the Romney and Denge Marsh Drains Catchment Board.[6] But, by 1989, erosion had resulted in near collapse of the structure. Large-scale reconstruction was required, and this was undertaken in two separate phases.

---

4. This is the original spelling, although the pits are sometimes shown as "Hoppen", and the name has also been corrupted to "Open" by a number of sources, including the Ordnance Survey.
5. A local name for the area between Galloways and Jury's Gap.
6. Later taken over by the Kent Rivers Catchment Board (and subsequently Kent Rivers Authority).

The current Dungeness outfall, under construction in 1990 (Photo courtesy David Read)

The first involved the strengthening of pipes at the seaward end and construction of the concrete outfall. Shortly after (from 1990 to early 1991), the more landward pipes to this new outfall were replaced with box culverts.[7] The strange landward arrangement of the long culvert with air release upstands is far from usual and is designed to prevent shingle from entering and blocking the watercourse for some distance upstream. However – and inevitably – the erosion has continued and, to prevent major flooding, a further landward outfall will be required in the near future.

The outfall can be reached by a track that redefines the meaning of "pot-holed" or, on foot, along the shore in front of the power station. The latter approach is probably more dramatic, because it takes you over tracts of shingle that have very little vegetation and which provide an interesting comparison with the eastern part of the 'Ness. There are numerous reasons for this: the prevailing wind (with no protection offered by the power station building); the severe damage inflicted during the war (through shelling); and the disruption resulting from the building of the power station itself. To the west, too, ongoing army activity on the Lydd Ranges has ensured that there is precious little vegetation anywhere near the beach. This helps to make the contrast with the route of the Dengemarsh sewer all the more striking. For, resulting from the regular supply of non-salt water into which plants with longer root systems can tap, this appears as a lush valley amidst the sea of shingle.

---

7. The first phase of the scheme was undertaken by Brett Paving and Construction (Canterbury); and the second (which was more complex) by contractor May Gurney of Colchester.

1. Overview – The (Un)Natural Landscape & Its Colonisation

The Dengemarsh sewer and outfall shown on a map of 1940 (left; when there was also a house and even a pub nearby – extract used with kind permission of Ordnance Survey); and its highly colonised environs in 2017

The southern end of the Dengemarsh sewer, which at this point runs underground. The building in the left background is the Dengemarsh lookout

Flora

Given its initial infertility and harsh conditions, it seems counter-intuitive that a third of the land area is now covered in vegetation, and that more plant species can be found here than in any other part of the country. In fact, 600 different types of plants grow at Dungeness, a third of all species present within the United Kingdom. This, in turn, contributes to an environment that supports many rare species of butterflies, moths, bees, spiders and beetles.

Where the shingle closest to the sea is concerned, the key to plant colonisation is sea kale. Although susceptible to trampling, this is an incredibly hardy and adaptable plant, which has managed to become established on many dry shingle beaches. Its seeds are also resilient and are borne on the sea. At the highest tides, these are deposited on to the shingle beach and may also be blown further onshore, taking them above the high tide line. The sea kale has a strong root system, which reaches down as far as three metres to search out water deposits and provides an anchor against the strong winds that characterise this part of the coast. In addition, the plant has coarse, waxy leaves, which both absorb any available moisture and resist water loss, another feature that makes sea kale an excellent colonising agent.

Once sea kale has been established on the outer (seaward) shingle ridges, conditions are created that are more conducive to other plant life. The dying plant provides organic matter and nutrients that allow others to gain a foothold; lichens are particularly quick to seize on such an opportunity and are highly important in the colonisation process. Pink and white valerian are early colonisers too, and provide a striking contrast to the green sea kale on the beach in early summer. Through the same process of growth and decay, conditions are established for other species.

Further back from the shoreline, the ridges or "fulls" provide minor geological and climatic differences between the sheltered troughs or "lows" (where the stones tend to be coarsest) and the tops of the ridges, where the shingle is smaller. Even such small differences provide microhabitats that can encourage plant growth, although species are still dependent on the availability of fresh (rather than saline) water. This is not as rare as might be envisaged, as the shingle does retain both rainwater and dew to a certain depth. This facilitates the spreading out of vegetation from the shore in a fairly regular pattern, with sea campion commonly the next species to colonise, followed by curled dock, common sorrel and (further inland) false oat and sweet vernal grasses.

Another plant to be found on the shingle further from the shoreline is broom. This flourishes on the older and more sheltered inland ridges and plays a key role in supporting further colonisation. Over a period of up to 20 years, the core of the plant dies down, leaving a sheltered space, which becomes filled with organic and decaying matter. This allows more specialised plants such as the Nottingham catchfly, sheep's bit and English stonecrop to take a hold. Furthermore, the root system and denseness of growth allows soil particles to be caught and retained whilst the plant itself increases the levels of humus, which in turn provides conditions for more growth.

1. Overview – The (Un)Natural Landscape & Its Colonisation

These two photos (from 1932 and 2017) demonstrate just how vegetation has become established over 85 years or so. The property in the centre of both pictures is South View

Campion (left) and sea kale (right) at Dungeness. In the autumn, the seed heads of the sea kale can be seen blowing across the shingle in vast quantities and have been mistaken for American tumbleweed

The process by which plants become established is therefore both complex and delicate, and any disruption to the shingle can have far reaching consequences. Whilst surviving photographs show a lack of vegetation in the early 20th century, they do not provide a complete picture. Although there is little historical evidence to prove it (prior to the era of widespread access to photography and at a time when Dungeness attracted little public interest), the likelihood is that the area was previously vegetated. However, once man started to make his mark, he changed the environment significantly.

One of the ways in which this was manifested was "clean beaching". In the same way that the 20th century suburban housewife would spend hours each week cleaning her front step in a show of pride, so her Dungeness counterpart would busy herself removing any weeds or plants from her garden or space surrounding the house. Of even greater significance was the huge negative impact that grazing had upon the vegetation and natural balance. Whilst, in the first half of the 20th century, only small numbers of cattle were kept (and these mainly on the

Nanny Goat Island

Galloways side of the Point), sheep were much more in evidence. Many were generally owned by farmers in the Lade, Greatstone and Littlestone areas, who would transport them to Dungeness and let them wander back home, grazing all the way. This practice would continue right up until the 1960s (when the power station was built).[8] Domestic goats – of which more later – would have an even larger impact on plant life.

More recently, the disturbance of the ground resulting from gravel extraction has created conditions that allow other species – such as ragwort, yellow horned poppy, vipers bugloss, red valerian, gorse and bramble – to take a hold. And the disused low railway embankment has become home to further species, particularly wood sage. Further plants of interest now to be found on the 'Ness include sea lavender and sea milkwort. There are many unusual mosses and lichens growing here, too, and worthy of special note is the reindeer moss (reinemusse), more usually found in alpine tundra.

Whilst the fresh water pits at one time supported a unique sedge-rich marshland, this has more recently become overtaken by salix (a form of willow). Greater silting, alongside the actions of man in lowering the water table, has in turn resulted in changes to the mix of flora here.

In recent years, poppies have taken a hold in the area, providing some spectacular contrasts – something that greatly appealed to filmmaker Derek Jarman, who used them in some of his works (see also Chapter 11)

Over the past two decades, purple orchids have colonised parts of the shingle, particularly in the Pen Bars area. These are sometimes protected from the grazing of rabbits by the placing of small wire mesh cages around them.

---

8. From the late 1990s, RSPB has re-introduced sheep within its reserve, grazing there during winter months.

1. Overview – The (Un)Natural Landscape & Its Colonisation

Fauna

Dungeness is a paradise for ornithologists, botanists and entomologists. Many rare species of bird have been spotted here, and these are not confined to the RSPB reserve: the 'Ness is the first land that many migrant birds will have seen in a long time, and they can often be seen in springtime resting on power lines. Similarly, they may be seen gathering here in the autumn, preparing for the long journey back to warmer climes. "Star attractions" include bitterns, Slavonian grebes, purple herons, Dartford warblers, great egrets and bearded tits. More common, but still a welcome sight, are wheatear, smew and stonechats. Many less exotic species can be seen on the sea, particularly congregating around the "boil", the area surrounding the power station outfall, which attracts many varieties of fish. These species include cormorants and most gulls.

The Stonechat is generally to be found in heathland areas, but tends to favour the coast in winter months. This bird was photographed near the Long Pits

By the early 1950s, rabbits were threatening to overrun the area. Living in surface tunnels in the soft alluvial soil in the railway embankment and amidst the brambles and blackthorn, they thrived. Their vast numbers provided plenty of opportunities for shooting, snaring and digging them out. Some skilled individuals could catch 150 animals in a day (mostly in the Ballast Hole area) so, in addition to providing a much-needed boost to the fishing families' pots, incomes could be supplemented by selling "bags" for decent money – often at Ashford Market. The presence of so many rabbits, of course, attracted foxes – which were almost unknown here prior to the 1940s. These posed a serious threat to many families, not only in terms of their supply of free rabbit stew, but also because, up until the mid-1950s, many families kept chickens for both eggs and meat. The Prebbles at Pen Bars, for example, kept up to

50 of these birds, which free-ranged along the Dengemarsh Road. For a short time after WWII (between 1949 and 1956), the world-famous Lydd company Lyddite Chicks also reared some 200 hens in the same location, and these would be allowed to roam on the beach during daylight hours. Accordingly, there was a need to strenuously manage the fox population, and regular culls took place. The hunting of foxes became a popular "sport" and there are tales of over 80 being shot at Dungeness in a single day, as well as of individual shooting parties setting out from pubs in Lydd and returning with a "bag" of in excess of 30 animals.

With changes in social attitudes, and with chickens no longer being kept domestically, there is no longer any appetite to actively manage the fox population. Perversely, though, there are few foxes left anyway. The outbreak of myxomatosis in Britain decimated the rabbit population, and Dungeness was certainly not exempt. It is estimated that this horrible man-introduced disease – which arrived at Dungeness in 1953 – accounted for well over 90% of the rabbits here, and the population has never recovered. Mr Fox, therefore, has moved on to where pickings may be richer.

Brown hares were also once plentiful. Although their numbers have severely declined in recent years, they can still be seen – but not in great numbers. More prevalent are badgers, which have taken to making their setts under the remains of wartime concrete gun emplacements. Stoats and weasels are present, too, but rarely spotted. Pigmy shrews, common shrews and wood mice are all to be found, along with common lizards, grass snakes and various species of bat. Amphibians, particularly marsh frogs and newts, are here in some number – encouraged in many cases by the hollows created by exploded WWII ordnance. Included within these species is the great crested newt, which, nationally, has been declining in number. Offshore, there are regular sightings of harbour porpoises, and less regular visits by white-beaked dolphins.

Entomologists will point to the rich variety of moths, with species such as the Eyed Hawk and White Spot Moths resident here, and an immigrant species – the Silver Y – found nowhere else in the UK. Interesting insects associated with the area include mining bees and the gorse shield bug. Dungeness is also home to more species of bumble bee than anywhere else in Britain, and was chosen as the site for reintroduction of the short-haired bumblebee (*Bombus subterraneus*) to the UK. Once native to the UK and widespread across the south of England, the loss of its species-rich grasslands had resulted in this bee becoming quite rare from the 1960s. It had been last recorded in 1988 – at Dungeness – and was eventually declared extinct in 2000. From 2012, the reintroduction programme has been carefully managed, with the importation of queen bees from southern Sweden.

Human Occupation

Claims have been made that settlement of Dungeness may have taken place as early as 1700 BCE, but this is clearly speculative, based on perceptions of when human life could have been supported (in all probability through fishing) on the parts of the 'Ness that then existed. Another story of uncertain provenance is that a hermit lived here for many years in the 13th century. More scientific is the work by the Romney Marsh Research Trust that confirms that fishermen were recorded at Dungeness in the mid-14th Century. There is also a written record of fisherman Thomas Inglott bequeathing his tenement and a "cabon"[9] to his wife in 1510; and evidence of a small chapel dedicated to St Mary existing at about the same time.

The construction of the first lighthouse in 1615 provides a further reference point; we also know that, prior to this, fires had been lit on the beach by locals to warn sailors. Inevitably, though, there were others – less public spirited – who sought to live off the misfortunes of others and were involved in the dark art of wrecking. One of the ships that met an unfortunate end after being lured onto the beach by wreckers was the *Alfresia*. Although there is debate as to the exact timing of its demise, this would appear to have been around the 1630s. It is commonly believed that part of this vessel became incorporated within the fabric of the original Pilot Inn, also suggesting that there were sufficient inhabitants to support a beerhouse of some size at this time.

Matthew Poker's 1640 map of Romney Marsh shows "the cabins"[10] at Dungeness, which were in all probability used by fishermen from Lydd during the herring season. These were on the eastern side of the Point, where the first of the fishermen's cottages that we would recognise as such today would later appear. There is a sound reason for this: the eastern shore still affords some limited shelter from the predominant south-westerly winds, and also allows greater protection than the western shore when launching boats from the steep shingle banking. Archaeologists have calculated how far inland these early buildings would have been, and

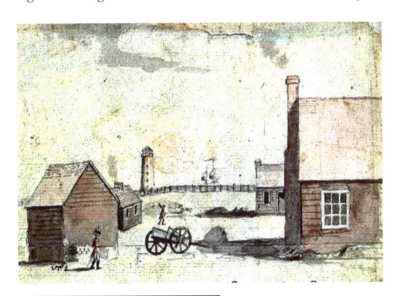

Dungeness in 1794, showing the third lighthouse and military barracks (built during the French Revolutionary / Napoleonic Wars)

---

9. A half-tenement.
10. The terms "cabin" and "cabon" would appear to have been interchangeable at this time.

made great efforts to find evidence of them, but with no success. This is in all likelihood due to the cabins having been of a very temporary nature, comprising materials to hand such as jetsam and easily-transported light resources from the locality.

The geography of the 'Ness has always made it vulnerable to enemy invasion and, towards the end of the 18th century, defensive preparations brought an influx of military personnel to the village; but, by then, the fishing community that would come to characterise Dungeness had become quite established. Regardless, Joseph Castle's poem (see frontispiece) demonstrates that Dungeness remained pretty wild and untamed in 1887. A cart track, which remained impassable for much of the winter, was the only real means of access from any direction prior to the coming of the railway.

There is debate over when the iconic fishermen's cottages that survive today first appeared, but it seems that a number were probably in place by the early 1860s, at the extreme northern end of the village.[11] There has been a suggestion that the former Pearl Cottage[12] existed in the 18th century, but this does seem unlikely. Most of the existing cottages were built between 1900 and 1920, and some were even constructed from driftwood. Many of these have been modified over the years, whilst still retaining a similar outward appearance. Between 1910 and c. 1925, eight or so properties were constructed by George ("Jerry") Bates and his brother Graham. These are at the southern end of the fishing beach, although still to the north and east of the Point. They include Spindle Cottage, Delhi Cottage, South View, East View, Beach Cottage and the Cabin.[13] Garden Cottage, home to members of the Tart family is believed to be the longest established of the surviving fishing cottages.[14]

Unrealised plans to construct a major port at Dungeness meant that the village received a railway service in 1883[15] but, whilst this brought some benefits to the fishermen in terms of the marketing of their catch, it did not materially alter the demographics in the short-term. This situation would change in the 1920s, however, when the Southern Railway authorised its staff to purchase redundant carriages and allowed them to be used as dwellings on their land. This heralded the start of the development of the southern end of the village, which had previously been the preserve of the Trinity House Lighthouse service, signal station and coastguard staff. At first, these carriages were treated as holiday homes, but some families soon moved in on a permanent basis. The transition was not a smooth one, as there was understandable tension between the established fishing community and the newcomers.

---

11. Although even these were probably preceded by the Watering House.
12. Now Pobble House.
13. Delhi Cottage, South View and East View were all built to the same specification. Lease records suggest that they date from 1911.
14. Although some claim that Garden Cottage dates from the 1850s, it seems more probable that it was built by Graham Bates only shortly before WWI. It is likely (from estate records) that it replaced an earlier building on an adjacent sit. It features on the cover of a Pink Floyd album, as well as in an episode of TV's *Inspector Lindley Mysteries*.
15. See Chapter 7.

1. Overview – The (Un)Natural Landscape & Its Colonisation

Garden Cottage (left), believed to be the longest established of the surviving fishing cottages, and Sea View (right), another of the older fishing homes in the north of the village

Despite the many strange twists which had determined the shape of Dungeness to this point, the most dramatic was yet to come. In 1956, the building of a nuclear power station here was first mooted; and, after work started in 1960, electricity generation finally commenced in 1965. Although this has now closed, the building remains (in line with decommissioning requirements), and its successor (Dungeness B) continues its work. This ensures that the site still dominates the flat landscape around it – particularly at night when, illuminated, it has been compared to an alien spacecraft. Additionally, it continues to be the largest employer in the area – with all the associated economic and demographic impacts.

The power stations have also exerted a powerful influence over nature. The initial construction work, the erection of their huge buildings and their continued existence have resulted in a large loss of habitat over the years, along with more traffic, greater human disturbance and increased lighting of the area. The pumping of water and nutrients back into the

sea has also created a specialised marine microhabitat. A wider impact has been from the line of large pylons feeding the national grid. In its early days, the number of fatalities resulting from birds crashing into the wires was described by the RSPB as "frightening".

Today, there remain many pointers to Dungeness's rich history and the ways in which it has been influenced by man, which this narrative seeks to explore. Most of the iconic railway carriage homes can still be identified and, whilst the tensions between the original owners and the fishing families may have disappeared, these have been replaced by mistrust of some of those who have more recently bought second homes here and distorted the housing market.

2

Fishing – A Way of Life

Despite everything else that has happened to, in and around Dungeness, it is the fishermen who have done most to shape both its history and its human geography. Although the delicate balance may now be changing irretrievably, the fishing community has very much moulded its culture and way of life. The same community is also responsible for the fascinating industrial archaeology that so characterises Dungeness Beach, and which has become a magnet for photographers.

Dungeness beach scene. The decaying structure (centre) is believed to be Len Prebble's former net shed

The families that have become synonymous with fishing at Dungeness first start appearing in official records from the mid-19th century. The first of these was the Tarts, who had been displaced from the Brooks and initially moved to Galloways, when the former was requisitioned by the army in 1865. They are reported to be descended from Huguenots fleeing France (Tarte[1] being the original name), and were joined soon after by the Oillers, an already-established fishing family, who moved here from Cornwall.

There were fishermen at Dungeness prior to the Tarts and Oillers, but it was these two families that breathed new life into the community. More organised and disciplined than their neighbours, they were also skilled boat builders. Their approach to house-building utilised similar skills and was certainly very practical: their homes were constructed with smaller

---

1. Doris Tart has been quoted as saying that her maternal grandfather was Bongaurde Tarte, although some other family members have questioned this French connection.

windows to give better protection against the cold winds; and, with the same goal in mind, driftwood from the beach was piled up against the outer walls. The Tarts and Oillers were soon joined by the Richardsons, the Thomases[2] and the Haines. In keeping with the majority of fishermen, these families occupied the eastern shore, to the north of the village – for reasons explained in Chapter 1. It should be recorded, however, that there was not a complete absence of fishing activity elsewhere. Although the tip of the Ness was considered too dangerous for the launching of boats, the area known as Pen Bars was favoured by a few hardy souls, who also constructed dwellings of varying quality and resilience. Three fishermen's properties were initially built here and the hamlet would come to be dominated by the Prebble and Freathy families, who were heavily involved with the Dungeness community for much of the 19th and 20th centuries. At the outbreak of WWII, four fishing boats were still being launching from the beach at Pen Bars; but fishing from here was abandoned during hostilities, and only briefly resumed thereafter.

The Prebble family's choice of location for their dwellings made much logical sense: close to the Dengemarsh sewer, it allowed the sinking of a well, which did not need to be dug to any great depth, meaning that rudimentary gardens could also be cultivated. Furthermore, being close to the well-established track to Lydd brought trading benefits.

The fact that there was once a pub – the Hope & Anchor – next door to the Prebbles' home should not be taken to imply that the Pen Bars was more widely populated. Pubs in the 19th and early 20th centuries were not the institutions we know today.[3] The Prebbles may have had more than one property, although it is more likely that generations lived in the same house (Myrtle Cottage), with some also occupying the Hope & Anchor. Len Prebble was born in Myrtle Cottage in 1904 and recorded that, from the age of six, he would walk the mile and a half each way from home to school across the shingle on a daily basis – unaccompanied, in all weathers, and often in the dark. It seems that Myrtle Cottage was rebuilt at least once, and the last family house was constructed here between the wars. This was a reasonably substantial affair, but was bulldozed when the army took over the area in 1945, extending the Lydd Ranges to better facilitate shelling practice.[4] Its concrete base, along with that of the Hope & Anchor, could still be seen in 2018. An unusual but touching memorial has been placed on the site, which is periodically graced with flowers.

The last of the remaining cottages on this part of the 'Ness was the Freathy family home, Spindle Cottage.[5] This was, unfortunately, destroyed in the early 1960s, to make way for the power station.

---

2. Claims have been made that the Thomases were amongst the original fishing families, althiugh this is hard to verify. They certainly also made a huge impact.
3. This is explored in more depth within Chapter 10.
4. The Prebble family then moved to the main Dungeness fishing enclave.
5. Spindle Cottage had been built at the same time, and to the same specification, as Garden Cottage (see Chapter 1). Althiugh referred to as Spindrift Cottage by a number of sources, it does seem that Spindle was the original name.

2. Fishing – A Way of Life

The distinctive memorial to the last Prebble dwelling at Pen Bars. The caption reads: "Myrtle Cottage Pen Bars Home to Steve, Millie, Doris & Len 1923 - 1945 at beloved Dengemarsh always home to Len Prebble Last Beachman of Dungeness"

The lonely Spindle Cottage, pictured in 1958, shortly prior to demolition to facilitate the building of the power station (photo courtesy Ted Carpenter)

The old fishermen's dwellings still comprise the bulk of the houses at the northern end of the Dungeness estate, and some retain the characteristics that demonstrate their credentials, particularly the distinctive net lofts reached by outside ladder. To most, it is these dwellings rather than the slightly newer railway carriages to the south, that best encompass the true spirit of Dungeness. As noted in Chapter 1, a number of the southernmost of these properties were constructed by George and Graham Bates, whose roles in the development of the area have never been properly recognised. Graham was the builder, who developed his own

Ferndale (left) and Ocean View cottages, both prominently displaying access to a net loft. Ocean View was built in 1915, at a cost of £175

company at Lydd.[6] He was keen to join his family at Dungeness, and even earmarked one property[7] for himself; unfortunately, his wife felt that life here would be too harsh and refused to move from Lydd. It was George Bates who provided the capital for the work, from the proceeds of his salvage and bunkering businesses. He really was a good friend to the fishing community, and rented to fishermen at low rates – waiving even these when catches were poor.

Most of the fishermen's properties are on the landward side of the coast road, although this road (replacing an earlier rough dirt track) was not constructed until 1938. Their distance from the sea demonstrates the extent to which the eastern side of the cuspate shore has continued to grow through the action of longshore drift, despite man's intervention. By way of further illustration, a former resident has spoken of the capstan for an ancestor's boat being just outside the back door in the 1890s. The family were landlords of the old Britannia Inn at the time, on a site right next to the RH&DR's Britannia points, and now some quarter of a mile from the sea.

Routines

Today, the availability of powerful modern motor vessels allows the fishing community access to fishing fields further away than hitherto, and more flexibility. But in the 19th and through-

---

6. The firm GH Bates would later take on much of the public building programme at Dungeness, too.
7. The Cabin, next to Spion Kop.

2. Fishing – A Way of Life

Garage Cottage, close to the current RNLI station, is another of the iconic Dungeness buildings erected by fishermen. Originally located near to the entrance to the Dungeness estate (and part of the former Pilot Inn), it did initially serve as a garage before being moved

out much of the 20th centuries, fishing followed a more regimented pattern. The onset of spring would signal the start of the plaice and sole season, which would continue into the summer. From late summer into the autumn, mackerel would be the main catch, but its harvesting presented its own specific dangers. For one of the forms of mackerel fishing involved entering the busy channel shipping lanes at dusk, to lay up to 750 metres of drift net at a time. The only protection that crews carried against tankers and other large ships would be a stock of paraffin-soaked flares.

By tradition, the herring nets would be brought down from the net lofts in late October, and these would have to be laced together and floats/bobbers attached in readiness for the next change of fishing season. Herring shoals could be unpredictable and their presence partly dependent upon weather conditions. Accordingly, if these fish were not present in sufficient numbers, the Dungeness fishermen would turn their attention to sprats. Sprats are significantly smaller in size, and therefore demand the use of finer nets. Offshore fishing was not, however, the only means of earning a living. In the days before commercial overfishing, stocks were very much higher and there was no legislation to limit the use of inshore netting. Ken Oiller (of one of the respected original families) very well captures the nature of these activities in his excellent booklet *Adventures of an Ordinary Dungeness Man*:

> There were two methods of onshore fishing: during the summer period, mackerel were in abundance and . . . one of the main methods was . . . known as Seine-netting. A net similar to a drift net would be anchored by rope to the beach, then four men would row-out with about 300 yards of net and create a half-circle. They would then wait about 15 minutes for the approach of a shoal – once the shoal had arrived within the

Charlie Richardson preparing his sprat nets (photo source: Ken Oiller's Dungeness Remembered*)*

catchment of the net the boat would be rowed back in a circular fashion to the beach and link up with the anchored rope ready to haul the catch in. This method of onshore fishing ceased to exist after the early 1950s.

The other method of onshore fishing was called kettlenet(ting).[8] It was a method known as "fishermen without boats". Drift-netting was not a successful method of fishing for mackerel during the summer, as the shoals keep very close to the shoreline. At low tide a row of poles were staked out on the foreshore and nets were hung from them, first in a straight line and then arranged to form a circular bight or pound. There was an inner and an outer bight/pound. When the tide came in the shoal of mackerel were funnelled into these circular entrapments. As the tide receded and the sea became low enough the men would wade into the bight and collect the fish. These poles and nets were erected for the duration of the summer months. . . . The heyday for this method of fishing was from 1890 up until the outbreak of WW2. Kettlenet fishing was finally phased out by the early 1950s.

For other workers at Dungeness – lighthouse keepers, military personnel, and coastguard staff – there was the promise of a regular wage. For fishermen, however, there was no such security. Although fishing remains a very hard way to earn a living, it was even harder in these years. Nowadays, if a fisherman is unable to put to sea for a few days, he is entitled to claim benefits; but this is a fairly recent initiative. Bad weather could keep a fisherman from going

---

8. This name derived from the action of the fish trying to swim out as the tide receded – their frenzy was akin to a kettle boiling. In some communities this became corrupted to 'keddlenet'.

2. Fishing – A Way of Life

Seine netting at Dungeness Beach (photo source: Ken Oiller's Dungeness Remembered*)*

to sea for days or even weeks at a time, and his family still had to be fed. In the severe winter of 1947/48, none of the fleet was able to put to sea for ten weeks. And, even if a good catch was landed, there was no surety of income; fish was despatched to Hastings or Billingsgate and was totally subject to market forces. It was not unknown for a note to come back from market to say that a whole catch remained unsold.

Accordingly, these hardy fishermen had to turn their hands to whatever opportunities presented themselves. These included shrimping and the digging of lug for sale (in addition to

The practice of boat kite fishing involved sending small unmanned boats out to sea attached to a kite. Baited hooks were attached and a rope kept it in touch with shore. More commonly associated with the USA and some other countries it is not believed to have been widely practised in the UK, but this exhibit at the Lydd Museum demonstrates that it was not unknown at Dungeness

that required for their own purposes) on nearby Greatstone or Littlestone beach. When conditions precluded going to sea, it was not only income that suffered: most of the families' staple diet was fish, too. In such circumstances, more primitive methods would be utilised to provide for the table: hooks would be attached to lines that were weighted with pebbles with a hole through them to catch fish; and, in the mackerel season, hooks were floated from sealed glass bottles, which were themselves floated on the sea. Not least, many fishermen additionally turned to the land, shooting rabbits, hares and wildfowl (geese, mallard and widgeon) to supplement the pot.

It should also be pointed out that risks to the fishing community have not been restricted to those of sea, weather and finance. Just occasionally, it is their catches that may be a problem. Some species of fish can inflict painful stings, but these, fortunately, are rarely fatal. A notable exception to this was recorded in May 1933, when William Robert Tart (landlord of The Pilot Inn) was mackerel fishing. He was stung by a weaver fish, prevalent in these waters. The sharp dorsal fins of the weaver always inflict painful stings, but in this case Tart suffered a bad reaction and died as a result.

Sons were expected to go to sea as soon as they left school (in many cases this would be before the official school leaving age). There was a strict understanding as to how the proceeds of the catch would be apportioned: whilst the vessel owner, skipper and crew would each take a full share of the profits, a boy would take only a half share until he reached the age of 18. He would thereafter take a three-quarter share until the age of 21 when, as a fully grown man, it was deemed that he was entitled to parity with his colleagues.

Equipment

There was rarely any real down-time for the fishermen and their families; there were always other things to attend to. A chore that was always top of the list was ensuring that the essential tools of their trade – their nets – were properly looked after.[9] Knotted, torn or even rotting nets could spell disaster, and much time was spent on maintenance.

In the days before synthetic material technology, it was necessary to treat the cotton nets to protect them from the sea water to which they would be exposed for long periods. This would be a task traditionally undertaken in the spring, when the nets were firstly placed in a tub full of linseed oil. They would then be hoisted up over a couple of tripods, with a bar across. Another bar would be pushed through the net to twist it out, wringing out as much oil as possible on the way. Once the nets had been dried on the beach, they would then be tanned in the kutch[10] copper before being laid out a final time on the beach for drying. After

---

9. Contrary to popular belief, these were not usually constructed locally. Most of the Dungeness fishermen used nets made to specification by a firm in Bridport, Dorset.
10. Kutch being an amber plant resin deriving from Burma (Myanmar) and Malaya (Malaysia).

2. Fishing – A Way of Life

One of the earlier tanning coppers (in use until the early part of the 20th century) has been restored and is another exhibit at the Lydd Museum

the nets had been processed in this way, items of clothing such as overalls and aprons would be similarly treated.

The type of copper used in this operation was superseded by a more robust brick version, which allowed the tanning solution to be boiled to a much higher temperature. The introduction of pre-treated nets, in the 1920s, in turn greatly reduced the use of such coppers, and the availability of nylon nets after WWII brought about their final demise – at the same time slightly improving the quality of life for the fishermen. Nevertheless, two excellent examples of the brick coppers have been preserved on Dungeness beach. The older of these was built in 1910 for the Tart family, in whose ownership it still remains. It is Grade II listed, and larger than most of its kind. The other, dating from 1920, was restored as one of the projects to celebrate and commemorate the new Millennium.

Other infrastructure

Vessels were traditionally launched and pulled back up the beach by hand, although a few boat owners did construct wooden capstans. Following the withdrawal of the army after WWII, the vast array of machine parts left behind resulted in the creation of more robust, metal winches. Over time, these were replaced by motor-driven versions.

The work of the fisherman did not, of course, end with the landing of the catch. Prior to the coming of the railway, fish would be taken by horse and cart to New Romney, Lydd or further afield to Folkestone and Hastings. With the opening of the railway in 1881, the bulk of the catch would still be sent to Lydd, but mainly for onward transmission to Billingsgate Fish Market.

The restored 1920 tanning copper (above), which is located slightly to the north of the 1910 example (top)

Examples of both wooden capstan and mechanical winches can still be seen on the fishing beach

Boat owners laid small-gauge railway tracks on the beach to connect with a common track, which would later link to the Admiralty siding. A good summary is provided by a descendant of the Bates family:[11]

> The rails at Dungeness came from Blackman the fish merchant from Hythe and we got some replacements from the army at Lydd camp. Before the estate road when the rails were put in there were rails across to the boats running at right angles to the shore. Up the inland end of each rail was a turntable thing, which turned your truck onto another line, which ran from approximately where the new Pilot is now to Spion Kop so you could bring your fish up to the road at the Pilot easily. That went when the estate road was put in, of course.

These tracks became known as "skipways", and some impressive research by Mike Trevett has identified that there were at least ten of these in use at various times. The majority were of 2 foot gauge, but three were of only 15 inches. It is likely that these, too, started life with a wider span, but that the availability of surplus wagons from the 15 inch Romney, Hythe and Dymcurch Railway (RH&DR) prompted a change. Sections of decaying skipway line remain an iconic sight on the fishing beach today.

A further line may have run in front of the fishermen's cottages for a short distance, just above the line of high water and connecting to the RH&DR near the Pilot Halt. This is by no means certain, however, and is considered in more detail within Chapter 7 (which also discusses some other short stretches of tramway that may have been involved in the movement of fish).

The line (to Spion Kop) was, by all accounts, constructed by Charlie Richardson, and is presumably that visible in this picture (just left of centre, behind Beach Cottage), taken from Spion Kop (1932)

---

11. This is Paul Copson, great grandson of George Bates, and grandson of Mick.

Most of the tracks constructed for transporting fish from the shore to road/Admiralty sidings were of two-foot gauge (as left). The one on the right is 15 inch, changed to accommodate wagons purchased from the RH&DR

Community spirit

It is hardly surprising that the remoteness of the area, allied to the precariousness of the fishing industry, bred a special kind of closeness and community spirit. This is partly manifested in the designation of nicknames to all who formed a part of it. These would usually reflect a particular specialism or skill, although some bestowed upon children would remain for life. Such names have included: Gritter Oiller (who, as a child, would be tasked with collecting grit to add to the chickens' feed); Choke-em Oiller; Darky Tart; Butcher Richardson; Tubber Bates; Gender Oiller (presumably, according to his son, because he fathered children of different genders); Tibbles Brignall; Punch Tart; Brown Tart; Honker Haines; Cholley Joe Oiller (aka Joe Bean); Treacle Richardson; Chaplain Richardson; Patchy Oiller; Nutty Oiller; Musher Croft; Trimmer Croft; Beefer Thomas; and Leather Jacket/Old Jerk (Jack Ford). Properties were also more commonly known by the name of their owner, with Spion Kop known as "Jerry's" (George Bates's nickname), Prospect Cottage as "Char's" (Charlie Richardson's) and East View as "Brown's".

This community spirit also manifested itself at Christmas, when a few of the more musically inclined fishermen and their wives would dress as minstrels in what could be best described as romper suits, and apply makeup before travelling from house to house, entertaining their neighbours. The custom was that they would be rewarded with a drink at each house, with the inevitable result that, by the time The Pilot (the final destination) was reached, the musicians could barely stand. Other eagerly anticipated Christmas traditions included the men challenging the womenfolk to games of tug-of-war and football. For a number of years from the 1970s, there was also an annual May Day celebration, which embraced a number of different activities

2. Fishing – A Way of Life

Christmas minstrel (left; photo courtesy Steve Tart); and a May Day celebration: Ken Oiller and his son-in-law performing their own anti-rain dance (from Ken Oiller's Tales of an Ordinary Dungeness Man*)*

– although often degenerating into a drunken but good-natured and endless pub crawl between The Pilot and the Britannia – where a hog-roast would be a major attraction.

There were few creature comforts for the early fishermen and their families: telephone and electricity were late to arrive at Dungeness, and mains water was laid on only in 1946. Up until then, water mostly had to be drawn from hand pumps, the most heavily used being that sited about 30 yards from Pleasant Cottage (on the landward side).[12] Most families would use a traditional yoke, with pails hanging from either end, to fetch supplies. Toilet arrangements were very basic – children learnt from an early age to stand upwind when emptying the latrine bucket on the beach! But the lifestyle also bred ingenuity; a clear example of this was the development of basic but imaginative footwear for negotiating the shingle. This essentially comprised the use of wooden blocks with a leather strap, slipped over shoes or boots and known as backstays, a word that would sometimes be shortened to "baxter". These worked on a similar basis to snowshoes on snow, and experienced users could develop quite a speed (and, for many years, a backstay race formed an integral part of the Lydd Club Day entertainment). Backstays were also very responsive, helping the wearer to keep to worn tracks across the shingle in the dark.

In similar vein, sledges were constructed from wooden boxes or beer barrels with runners attached, to assist the movement of fish across the beach prior to the laying of railway track (or in its absence). Inevitably, these would also be commandeered by the children to slide down the steep shingle banks into the sea in the summer months.

The same mentality ensured that anything washed ashore that was salvageable was used – and considered to be fair game. There are shades of the film *Whisky Galore* at work here, and

---

12. Some fortunate families did have a pump on their own premises (usually in the kitchen), but they were the exception. The RH&DR installed a wind pump (clearly visible in many postcards) to bring up water from a deep-level lake, and this was not dismantled until 1951.

An assortment of backstays and a fish sledge (both photographed at Lydd Museum)

a number of stories are told of various attractive cargoes being "liberated". One of these was, indeed, a consignment of whisky, which started to appear on the beach in the late 1960s. Alert to the impending interest of the authorities, many cases were buried deep under the shingle. When the furore had died down, however, it is recounted that the fishermen were unable to locate the bulk of their booty!

Two further incidents are again related by Ken Oiller:[13]

> Once a huge cask of sherry was washed ashore. Of course it was the duty of the local inhabitants to inform the Customs Officers of any such valuable items, but this was too good an opportunity to miss. I can still see my father trudging across the shingle with two pails hanging from the yokes across his shoulders. When chests of tea washed ashore on the point and along the western beach, my brother and I dragged our little sledge – made from a box with barrel staves fixed to the bottom – along the beach. We filled it with tealeaves and took it home to mum.

In similar fashion, in January 1931 a collier (bulk cargo ship carrying coal)[14] broke its back just off the Ness. Such was the extent of the damage that it had to be towed away in two pieces, with none of its load remaining. The whole coastline between Littlestone and Dungeness turned black, and it was widely said that the Lydd coal merchant very nearly went out of business!

It is easy to understand the morality involved here. The government provided very little to the inhabitants of Dungeness by way of services, so why should there be any goodwill on the part of the fishing families? Accordingly, payment of taxes was not always high on the local

---

13. *Dungeness Remembered.*
14. This was the *Nurturian*, a 10,000 ton steam ship.

agenda, and it was thus inevitable that some residents would also be involved in smuggling. This was not on the same organised level as at some other settlements along the coast (such as Dymchurch), but it was certainly condoned. And it was not confined to the 19th century either; post-WWII, the landlord of the Hope & Anchor pub was successfully prosecuted for his role in hiding smuggled goods.[15] In addition to smuggling and the recovery of goods washed up on the shore, it would seem that there was also some imaginative "recycling" of items of a more permanent nature. For example, it has been widely reported that, following the introduction of electricity to the village in the early 1950s, some of the lead supplied to encase the cables ended up as weights to hold down fishing nets!

Husbandry

Whilst the opening of the railway allowed most other essential goods to be brought in, there was still no daily supply of fresh dairy products. To counter this problem, many of the fishing families took to keeping goats. Much hardier than cows, goats could survive and even flourish on the rough grazing to be found inland from the dwellings, and most were allowed to roam freely. Some would become family pets and the children would often be given the exciting task of rounding them up each evening; but it was still a source of amazement and shock for casual visitors between the wars to find a large population of up to 80 untethered goats roaming the shingle. Dungeness, already viewed as a wild outpost, now acquired the nickname *Nanny-goat island*. The goats remained during WWII, but it was difficult to curb their roving

Two pre-war shots of domestic goats kept at Dungeness. Horace Sinclair (who lived at the property Caithness and was one of the first railway carriage inhabitants), is shown in the right-hand photo (Chris Shore collection)

---

15. See Chapter 4.

Mrs Joanna Thomas outside Lloyd's Cottage, with family dog and chickens (photo courtesy Peter Thomas)

habits. Unfortunately, the combination of free-range goats and a mined environment had inevitable consequences, with a number meeting a tragic and untimely death. With sick humour, the new nickname for Dungeness became – for a time – *The Land of the Exploding Goats*.[16] After the war, most families got rid of those goats that hadn't perished, although a few maintained the tradition (albeit now being required to keep them tethered), despite there no longer being a dependency on them for fresh milk.[17]

The keeping of chickens was more enduring and, whilst some were kept for meat, the vast majority were for eggs, but also serving as family pets.

The War Years

Surprisingly, WWII brought a small level of prosperity. It is not clear that fishing was a reserved occupation for the full duration of the war, but the Dungeness fishermen were exceptionally allowed to remain in their houses whilst other coastal residents were evacuated.[18] Because all larger trawlers had been commandeered for use as minesweepers, these fishermen

---

16. The goats were particularly attracted to the Ballast Hole area, where anti-tank mines were concentrated.
17. And, in the late 1970s, Sylvia Oiller brought two goats back to Beach Cottage as part of what was effectively a smallholding, with chickens, ducks and even turkeys. There are reports of some fishermen also keeping pigs pre-war, particularly at Pen Bars/Dengemarsh.
18. Many of the Dungeness fishermen showed their commitment to the war effort by enrolling in the local Home Guard. Others joined the Royal Observer Corps, looking out for suspicious activity in the Channel. Fuller details are provided in Chapter 3.

had far less competition than previously; and, although restrictions were imposed on access to the foreshore between sunset and sunrise, larger catches became commonplace. Furthermore, there was a controlled price on all species, which – at 14 shillings a stone – was a great improvement on many pre-war prices. There were also richer pickings to be had from what was washed up on the shore. Notable was the aftermath of the torpedoing of American liberty ship *Annie Oakley* in the west bay. In a strong flood tide, the vessel drifted past the end of Dungeness Point before finally sinking about two miles offshore; for weeks afterwards, tins of cigarettes and food washed ashore and were eagerly retrieved by fishermen and their families.

Not just for men?

Fishing is undoubtedly a hard profession, and has for long been considered a male-only occupation. Indeed, it has traditionally been considered bad luck to even allow women on the boats. Whilst there were some wives and daughters who did go to sea towards the end of the 20th century, a 1930 directory entry shows a Miss Caroline Gibbons of Pearl Cottage registered as a fisherman. It is puzzling that none of the established fishing families can recall stories of this apparent early blow for women's liberation. Other women would also turn a hand to shrimping, and even digging lug, when times were hard.

The current scene

Up until the 1960s, the Dungeness fishing boats would be spaced out along the beach between The Pilot Inn and Spion Kop, opposite the houses of their owners. By this time, however, fishing methods were beginning to change, with long-lining becoming more popular than trawling for a period. But even well into the 1950s and 60s, most fishermen kept two

The modern-day Dungeness fishing fleet (2016)

separate vessels, for trawling and for drifting. As recently as the 1980s, there was still a fleet of over 20 boats, but at the time of writing there are just four fishing vessels operating commercially from Dungeness beach – although these are huge in comparison to their predecessors. They are to be found in the area of the Old Boathouse – part of the former lifeboat station. (Note that, whilst there are other boats pulled up on the shingle, some of these are unused and others are manned by those who have alternative main employment. Still others are reserved for charter, mostly by groups interested in wreck fishing).

Local sales

Although, historically, the bulk of catches would be sent straight to market, from the time of the completion of the road to the Point, many of the local fishermen would sell a small proportion of their catches from their homes. This would commonly be in its natural state, but sometimes filleted.

There has, however, also been a regular local market for smoked or cured fish. At Dungeness, as with many coastal fishing communities along the coast prior to the mass availability of refrigeration, the traditional means of preserving fish was through curing.[19] For years, smoke holes or herring hangs satisfied this need and were used quite widely, even up to the end of the 1960s.[20] The tradition was revived in the 21st century, by former fisherman Jim Moate and his family. Moate had had to give up fishing due to a back injury, but was reluctant to sever his links with the sea. Finding some old recipes at his home at Pearl Cottage, and talking to some of the older fisherman who were familiar with the practice of curing, he determined to resurrect the practice. This resulted in a thriving local business for a couple of years, although Moate's laudable refusal to sell to restaurants or by mail order did restrict its potential. When he sold Pearl Cottage in 2008, the curing stopped and the smokery was later demolished to make way for the Shingle House.[21]

The family practice did continue, though, with Kess and Joldine Moate providing a similar but reduced service from Dunrunnin' (between the two lighthouses) for a short time; and a natural oak smoker is now utilised by M&M Richardson (see below).

Into the new millennium, with so few fishing boats operating full time from Dungeness Beach, opportunities for the public to buy direct have been greatly reduced. The enduring exception has been the Richardson family business (now named M&M Richardson), run from

---

19. The process of curing involves salting the fish before soaking them in a saltwater brine and then hanging them up to smoke over a low fire. This drives out the water and replaces it with a saline solution; the smoke then glazes the fish, "sealing" it so as to preserve the meat.
20. Unfortunately, none of the traditional herring hangs remain at Dungeness, although a very good example is preserved nearby, at Lydd.
21. Some excellent footage of the Smokery is contained within the Inspector Lynley television episode (see Appendix C). Chapter 11 contains more detail on the Shingle House.

2. Fishing – A Way of Life

The Dunrunnin' smokery

The Richardsons' fresh fish outlet (M&M Richardson, TN29 9NJ), next to the RH&DR line, in Battery Road

their shop at Sealight in Battery Road. This was founded by Harry Twosign[22] Richardson shortly after he returned from service at the end of WWII, to sell the fish and bait from his own labours. The decision to locate the shop in Battery Road still makes sound economic sense, as it attracts the passing trade as well as many of the tourists making for the estate. Harry's son, William, took over the shop but, with his death in 2010, the last of the family fishing boats was sold off. The business has survived, however, with grandson Mark now at

---

22. This unusual name was given to a number of men in the Richardson family. It apparently recalls a foreign shipwreck survivor, who swam towards the shore after his ship was wrecked off Dungeness, and took the surname of the man who pulled him from the water. On one marriage certificate, it is spelt "Tosine". Since his time, so many members of the family have occupied houses in Battery Road that it is known to many locals as *Richardson Row*.

The Snack Shack, pictured on a busy May lunchtime, 2018

the helm (it is his and wife Marion's initials that appear over the door). The shop continues to sell locally caught fish, but also makes home deliveries and has diversified by additionally selling fishing tackle.

In 2014, members of one of the other remaining fishing dynasties – the Thomas family – determined to arrest the decline of fish sales on the estate, opening the Dungeness Fish Hut and Snack Shack, co-located next to Doreen Thomas' cottage (Way O' the Wind). The family has two beach-launched catamaran fishing boats, one of which – in deference to their well-known and popular matriarch – is called *The Doreen T*. The family had sold fish from the beach for many years in the past, but it had got to the point where age was catching up with Doreen and the menfolk, all tied up on the boats, were rarely able to help out. It was only when son Kenny felt no longer able to carry on out at sea that the new business came into being. Kenny's daughter Kelly Smith, a serving police officer looking for a change of career so as to be able to spend more time with her children, also saw an opportunity. She was less keen on the wet fish sales side but used her creativity and her experience of the London street food scene to establish the Snack Shack. Since then, she has recruited her cousin, Sarah, as business partner.

The Snack Shack has been featured in national newspapers and magazines, and been shortlisted in the Best Coastal Fish Restaurant of the Year awards. Its proud boast is that many of its products are so fresh that they were swimming in the sea earlier the same day! It is an unprepossessing affair, essentially an old shipping container surrounded by an assortment of picnic tables – yet in many ways it perfectly typifies the pragmatic approach that Dungeness people have to life. The climate is not always conducive to *al fresco* dining, so a supply of blankets is made available to customers. Cushions are also provided on request, but on hot summer days, demand inevitably outstrips the supply of seats and tables; so deckchairs, lobster pots and anything else that can be found on a working fishing beach are pressed into service! This all adds to the wonderful ambience of the venue. In its short existence to date, the Snack Shack has provided a much-needed service, and draws many additional people to the area.

3

Defence of the Realm – Wartime

The location of Romney Marsh long ago earned it the tag "the invasion coast", and control of the Channel has been paramount in terms of national defence. In this context, Dungeness has held pivotal strategic importance. As early as 1652, the most significant Dutch victory of the first Anglo-Dutch War – which saw a fleet under Maarten Trump gain temporary control of the English Channel – was the Battle of Dungeness. But it was the Napoleonic Wars that really concentrated governmental minds and resulted in the implementation of more formal systems of coastal monitoring and defence.

Napoleonic Wars

By the end of the 18th century, the French Revolution had thrown much of Europe into panic and turmoil. Napoleon Bonaparte was proving to be a real threat, and Britain anticipated an invasion attempt. Essentially, the physical land-based defensive measures implemented to counter the Napoleonic threat can be split into three categories, by size. Batteries were the first line of defence, and the keystone of these fortifications. Although varying in size, they were self-contained structures with a raised terreplein[1] to afford a command of the sea. There were 11 of these batteries built between Deal and Eastbourne, of which seven were on the Romney Marsh coast. Three were at Hythe, but the other four were sited between Lade and Dungeness – in recognition that this was the most likely point of attack. Batteries were supplemented by Martello towers constructed at strategic points (although there were none at Dungeness), and larger fortifications known as redoubts. Redoubts date from mediaeval times; literally "places of retreat", they were initially independent earthworks built within a permanent fortification to reinforce them, their chief purpose being to protect soldiers outside the main defensive line. They became more popular during the colonial era, but after that, were mostly constructed from stone or brick.[2]

No.1 Battery, Battery Road

Both Number 1 and Number 2 Batteries carried the Dungeness suffix, although the latter was

---

1. The top platform or horizontal surface of a rampart on which guns are mounted.
2. The redoubt is not to be confused with the redan, as the latter was open at the rear.

Nanny Goat Island

a mile and a half further down the coast at Lade.[3] Although most histories show that the majority of batteries and redoubts date from 1798, Battery No 1 was probably built in 1793 or 1794.[4] Despite not being as well preserved as its counterpart,[5] it is not too difficult to locate its remains, as the address provides a large clue: it is sited in what is helpfully named Battery Road, almost opposite the entrance to the Dungeness estate, and just over a mile north of the old redoubt. It is widely believed (although difficult to confirm conclusively) that it was known to soldiers as Moore's Fort. If so, then this could have been a reference either to Lt General Sir John Moore (who commanded the Shorncliffe Barracks from 1803), or a subaltern in charge locally.

Two views of what was formally known as Dungeness No. 1 Battery. The above photo dates from 1910; and that on the left was taken a few years later. In the latter, the first lifeboat station can be seen, centre background (both photos courtesy Ted Carpenter)

3. The numbering of these batteries appears quite counter-intuitive, but it is likely that it reflects the different dates of construction.
4. Records show Captain Samuel Finn of the Lydd Volunteers being appointed barrack master here in 1794, although they do not indicate whether he was the first holder of that post.
5. Lade Fort is the best remaining example of all the original batteries.

3. Defence of the Realm – Wartime

In 1860, long after the Napoleonic threat had passed, the battery was remodelled and reinforced to accommodate five heavier guns. Disused by the end of the 19th century, it does seem that it may have been re-occupied during WWII, as Nissen huts are visible on aerial photos taken of the site in 1946 (although other evidence – due in part to the area being declared a restricted area – is again lacking). It certainly served as a storage area for the PLUTO project at this time (see later in this chapter).

In the 1960s, as part of an initiative to tidy up the area, Kent County Council started to demolish the structure. Intervention by local historians Anne Roper and Ted Carpenter, however, managed to prevent its complete destruction, and there is still enough of it remaining to make for an interesting site visit.

A reasonable proportion of the walls and gun emplacements of Battery No. 1 still remaining in 2014 (left), along with a plaque providing a brief history of the site (right)

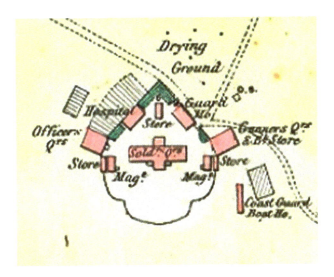

Plan of No. 1 battery, Dungeness (copyright ownership unknown)

Nos 3 and 4 Batteries

Number 3 and 4 Batteries were constructed on the western side of Dungeness Point. They were both built of concrete and shingle with brick revetments to a fairly typical design, with a brick loop-holed wall three and a half metres high extending from the corners to form a sharp point at the rear, providing defensive protection. The main entrance, guardroom and ancillary buildings were spaced along the exterior walls.

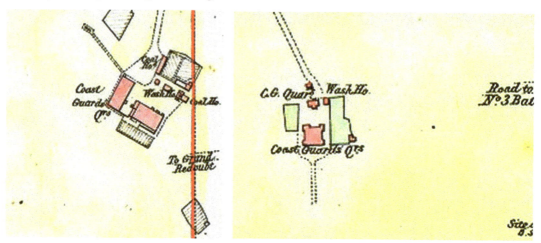

Plans of No. 3 (left) and No.4 (right) Batteries, as they were in 1867 (copyright ownership unknown)

Four 24-pounder guns were mounted on traversing platforms in a faceted arc, facing the sea. As with most of their counterparts, these batteries were each manned by three officers and up to 50 non-commissioned officers and other ranks.[6] It is likely that they were constructed slightly after Battery No. 1 (probably in 1798, as discussed below). Both were destroyed by the sea some time between 1818 and 1823, and no traces remain.

Dungeness Redoubt

The redoubt[7] on Dungeness Point supplemented batteries 1, 2, 3 and 4. It was the first of the redoubts to be built on the Marsh, with work commencing in 1798 (the likelihood being that this was concurrent with work on Nos 2, 3 and 4 Batteries). An earthwork construction of octagonal design, it was some 600 feet in diameter and initially armed with eight 24-pounder guns[8] mounted around the ramparts.

---

6. The only known batteries not to conform to this norm were at Hythe, where larger structures accommodated up to 100 men.
7. This is referred to in records of the time as the Grand Redoubt. Current histories, however, suggest that the only "true" Grand Redoubt was that at Dymchurch – which was certainly much larger. The Dymchurch Grand Redoubt is the best surviving example of its type.
8. Some sources report that there were as many as 11 of these 24-pounders.

3. Defence of the Realm – Wartime

As an illustration of the rather woolly thinking that characterised the government's response to the threat of Napoleonic invasion, an investigation launched in 1803 found the Dungeness redoubt to be unfit for purpose. More specifically, the conclusion was that it was not defensible against a *coup-de-main*;[9] and neither could it be made so at any moderate expense!

The redoubt decayed over time, and what little remained was demolished in the 1950s. Against the flat landscape of Dungeness, however, the raised earthworks are still clearly visible.

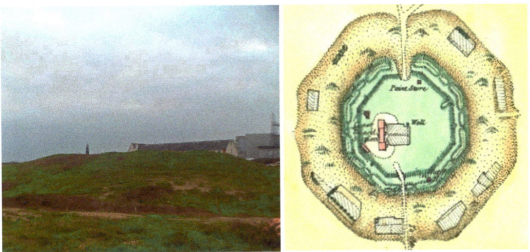

The surviving earth ramparts of the Dungeness Redoubt later became home to the RNSSS cottages (top picture, as seen from top of old lighthouse, 2016); bottom left – rear view from ground level. Bottom right – plan of Dungeness Redoubt (copyright ownership unknown)

---

9. The meaning of this phrase being: "by direct assault rather than by artillery".

Royal Naval Shore Signal Station (RNSSS) – to 1814

Also in response to the threat posed by Napoleon, in 1795 the Admiralty[10] authorised the construction of a chain of communication stations to maintain a watch against potential invasion. This (ironically) utilised the levered semaphore signalling system only recently developed by the French. The main criterion was for sites with good sight lines, both out to sea and along the coast. Although most were built on high land, Dungeness Point was one of 57 such "shutter" or shore signal stations established on the south coast between North Foreland and Lands End. This network allowed messages to be relayed quickly to the Royal Dockyards at Portsmouth, from where the fleet could be instructed. Land for this purpose was commandeered, but the landowner received rent and was promised the option of keeping the building when it was decommissioned. In most cases, the station building comprised a small prefabricated wooden structure with two rooms (one living accommodation for the Royal Naval lieutenant in charge; the other for the three seaman who made up the rest of the staff complement). The only equipment supplied was an 80-foot signal mast capable of flying flags and displaying signal balls; signals; and a code book. The staff maintained a constant watch and slept on site. Unfortunately, it is not known precisely where the first Dungeness Signal Station was sited. Given the good sight lines and proximity to the shore, it is possible that it was positioned on the land on which the redoubt would be built three years later. Certainly, it was later sited within the redoubt.

Whilst signal stations were deactivated following the Peace of Amiens in 1802, the failure to achieve a lasting peace meant that they were re-established in May 1803, and the location and proximity of the Dungeness station to the redoubt meant that it was identified as strategically the most important – thus becoming the best-equipped of all the stations or posts. At the end of 1803, however, Lt Corsellis (in charge of the Dungeness post) raised the concern that, in severe weather, visibility was severely restricted. As a consequence, a formal agreement was struck between the Admiralty and Trinity House by which the lookout staff could be accommodated on the top floor of the lighthouse when conditions demanded. A further agreement was later made between Lt Edger of the Signal Post and Captain Pole (in charge of the Dungeness redoubt) that, in the event of a French fleet being sighted in the Channel, guns would be fired three times from the redoubt. Other redoubts, on hearing this, would also fire three guns, thus passing the warning message by sound as well as sight.

The Shore Signal Stations continued in use until 1814, when the war against Napoleon was all but won. Just four years later, though, they were given yet another lease of life when redeployed in the fight against smuggling.[11] There is now a row of cottages inside the redoubt earthworks, and long-term RNSSS staff accommodation was probably first erected here

---

10. The term Admiralty for what we would now call the Royal Navy may cause some confusion. It survived in common usage until 1964, when the Admiralty formally became part of the Navy Department of the Ministry of Defence (MoD).
11. This and the subsequent history of the Signal Stations is explored further in Chapter 4.

3. Defence of the Realm – Wartime

around 1820. A number of current residents believe that they occupy the same buildings, albeit much altered and upgraded – but this is questionable. The cottages certainly resemble those built for the Coastguard Service between 1878 and 1905 (such as at the entrance to the estate, and at Lade and Littlestone) and it would seem likely that the same contractors may have been used to construct new RNSSS premises; however, the author has been unable to find definitive proof of this. Over the years, these cottages have also been variously used as accommodation for coastguard families;[12] for private housing; and by the Dungeness Bird Observatory (DBO). They are now part of the EDF estate; most are leased to families, but the DBO continues to occupy the end property and a number of their hides and nets (used to trap birds for ringing purposes) can be seen in the vicinity.[13]

The Watch House

The square building near the entrance to the Dungeness Estate, and now known as the Watch Tower, was constructed from an early form of concrete, using shingle from its environs. It is frequently claimed that its purpose was to provide an early warning of Napoleonic invasion. This may well have been the case, but the same sources also claim that it was manned by coastguards from the adjacent row of coastguard cottages. Given that the Coast Guard (as it was known in its early days) was not formally established until 1822, this cannot be factually correct. The coastguard cottages that stand today are of later vintage, dating from the late 1870s.

The modified Watch Tower, pictured in 2018 – with Coastguard cottages in the foreground

---

12. It is for this reason they are often referred to (wrongly) as the old coastguard cottages. More correctly they are the "former RNSSS cottages".
13. See also Chapter 9.

Some renovations to the Watch Tower have cut away part of the original construction to reveal the incorporation of local shingle in the cement (left). Despite being extended on three sides, the original tower remains and the stair rail (pictured right) has been brought in from the outside. It is possible that this formed part of the original building

Records indicate that the Dungeness Watch House was built in 1810, which strongly suggests a link to the Preventative Water Guard (PWG), which was formed in 1809 and was a forerunner of the Coast Guard service. As such, its primary purpose would have been to combat smuggling,[14] but it could have had a dual function, as already suggested (if it was used as a defence lookout during the Napoleonic wars, it would have been in tandem with the Signal Station, which had prime responsibility). The term Watch House was used generally for PWG accommodation, and the building was still known by this name in 1931. It was some time between then and 1952 that its owners changed this to the Watch Tower.

The original building has been much modified, particularly from the mid-1980s, but its earlier purpose is still evident. It now operates as a bed & breakfast establishment.

World War I

Given that there was no immediate threat to the south-east coast, activity on the Marsh in World War I was limited in the main to training exercises. There was little additional WWI defensive building work at Dungeness, although there was one significant exception. This was the construction of a fort, near to the site of the fog horn/low light (future site of the 1961 lighthouse), in 1914. There are few remaining photographs of this, although some that do exist are erroneously captioned to the effect that the structure was built as a defence against

---

14. See also Chapter 4.

3. Defence of the Realm – Wartime

Dungeness Fort (photo courtesy Ted Carpenter)

Napoleon. There are conflicting reports as to whether it was used or, indeed, even needed, in WWI, but the reality was that Admiralty guns were mounted here for at least the latter part of the conflict. It has also been suggested that there may have been early listening devices installed here for identifying submarine movements. Whilst this can't be confirmed, the design of the fort was unusual, which adds credibility to such claims.

Another structure that was used in the context of WWI was that known as the Old Revetments. Built in 1910, and thus predating hostilities, the revetments comprised targets and barricades against explosives, and featured heavily in the Royal Garrison Artillery practice and training routines. They stood on the edge of the coastline, just to the west of Dungeness Point, midway between the Dengemarsh outfall and the lighthouse. The Old Revetments are also shown on maps of the relevant period.

The Old Revetments, c. 1915

Casualties

WWI did not see as much conflict in the Channel as there would be in WWII, but there were still some notable casualties. On 8 February 1917, the tribal-class destroyer *HMS Ghurka*, serving as part of the Dover Patrol, hit a mine off Dungeness, with the loss of 74 of its 79 crew. Less than a year later, on 4 February 1918, another Dover Patrol vessel, *HMS Zubian*, sunk a German mine-laying submarine (UC-50) just off Dungeness Point.

World War II

Army/Admiralty Occupation

In the first few months of WWII, there were few outward signs that the country was at war. Once the German army started its march across Europe, however, Dungeness became transformed. The army took over the area, declaring it a restricted zone and introducing checkpoints. Only the fishing families were allowed to remain. Others were allowed to return periodically to check over their properties, but on condition that formal permission had been granted and that they first reported to the police station. The reasons behind this were brought into focus when a woman, who had received the necessary permission, omitted to contact the police in advance of entering what (in her case) was her holiday home. What she did not know was that the Royal Engineers had set a booby trap within. Military police, on being advised of activity inside, rushed to the cottage, fearing the worst. From outside, and via a megaphone, they instructed the woman to leave by the nearest door. It transpired that she had walked within inches of the trap and, when told of the danger she had been in, promptly fainted!

Warning sign displayed along the Romney Marsh coast advised of draconian penalties for committing crimes within restricted areas (left); and Lydd Road checkpoint, at the entrance to Dungeness by Halfway Bush (now the entrance to the power station), 1940 (photo courtesy John Wimble)

3. Defence of the Realm – Wartime

The army began fortification of the area with the arming of the existing (1914) Dungeness Fort. After significant reinforcement and enlargement (additional brickwork being added) in 1940, it was then used to accommodate both troops and six-inch guns. The officers' quarters were close by, on the site now occupied by the Britannia Inn. The fort later fell into disrepair, but survived *in situ* for a number of years after the war. There is debate as to the exact date, but what remained appears to have been demolished sometime around 1960.

Scaffolding was erected along the length of the beaches in a bid to delay any enemy tanks that might be landed, and gun pits were built at both Dungeness and Dengemarsh. The Royal Engineers laid an extensive network of mines, but a number were deemed to be too close to the lifeboat house for safety and a dispute then broke out between the Army and the Royal Navy (Admiralty) as to who should be in overall charge of the area. In this case, it was the Admiralty that won the battle, and the Army were forced to lift the mines. But, not having charted their positions, they were forced to try to detonate them one at a time; and, as the first one went off, the explosion triggered some 50 more. The resulting explosions shattered many windows and lifted the roof of the lifeboat house.

Conflict between the two services would remain for the duration of hostilities. The army next decided to commandeer the lifeboat house for use as a machine gun post, so more mines were laid and barbed wire erected. The Admiralty again had to intervene, to ensure that the lifeboat remained free to launch. The role of the lifeboat crew was even more fraught with danger at this time and, to add to their problems, the coxswain no longer had the final say over launching. This was now in the gift of the Admiralty, and the lifeboat crews were further concerned as to whether details of launches were properly passed on to other bodies – there being the additional risk that they would be mistaken for an enemy vessel and treated as such. Many locals joined the local Home Guard, and most boats within the fishing fleet were later issued with a .303 rifle; whilst two crews were also allocated a Bren gun.

There were plenty of other defensive measures put in place at Dungeness during WWII, although not all were formally recorded, and the secrecy of war spawned many rumours. One of the most enduring – and plausible – was that huge pits had been dug and filled with large boulders and detonators, with the intention of inflicting maximum damage to enemy troops in the event of a successful landing. Many sources also have it that microphones embedded in concrete rods were sunk into the beach to detect the presence of enemy submarines – using a similar principle to that of the sound mirrors at Greatstone.[15] There seems to be little evidence to support this, and it may be that there was confusion in relation to listening devices possibly once installed within the Fort (as previously related). Nevertheless, there are residents today who complain that vibrations from passing shipping are being picked up from these microphones, and that this affects their quality of life.

The Royal Observer Corp (ROC) took over the property Spion Kop, because its tower

---

15. These were part of a pioneering scheme that pre-dated RADAR, but which became obsolete with the development of the latter.

offered useful observation opportunities. An army patrol had clearly not been warned that the tower would be manned, however, and, when the occupants refused to respond to a challenge, opened fire on the ROC men, assuming them to be enemy agents. Luckily, no injuries resulted.

PLUTO

One of the most imaginative of the many WWII initiatives was the laying of undersea oil pipelines between England and France, principally to supply fuel to forces taking part in the 1944 Normandy landings. Allied forces on the continent required a huge amount of fuel to operate effectively, but bad weather often disrupted supplies carried by oil tanker. The tankers also increasingly became targets for the Luftwaffe and German submarines and so were later diverted to the Pacific conflict. There was real concern, too, that oil storage facilities located near the English Channel could be vulnerable to Luftwaffe attack. In response, Arthur Hartley, chief engineer with the Anglo-Iranian oil company, put forward the idea of using pipelines and, following trials in the Clyde and Bristol Channels, the first such line was laid along the bed of the English Channel from Shanklin Chine to Cherbourg, in August 1944. The second line to be laid was from Dungeness to Ambleteuse (near Boulogne).

The pipelines were the forerunner of all the flexible pipes subsequently used in the development of offshore oil fields, and that which entered the sea at Dungeness was 70 miles in length, running from Walton-on-Thames in Surrey, where it linked into the UK oil network. Where the pipeline crossed the marsh dykes, it was encased in concrete (producing excellent – if narrow – footbridges, some of which can still be seen today). To avoid detection by enemy planes, which flew frequent reconnaissance missions, the policy was to run the pipes adjacent to railway tracks wherever possible, and this was fully applied from Appledore to the coast. For similar reasons, the pipes were laid mostly at night, and great care was taken to cover any damage to vegetation.

The project was originally titled Pipeline Underwater Transport of Oil, but the rather magnificent acronym of PLUTO was born when a less cumbersome name (Pipe Line Under The Ocean) was coined. The codename for the section running between Dungeness and Boulogne was *Dumbo*, and that for the Isle of Wight to Cherbourg *Bambi*: clearly not acronyms, but following a theme none the less!

Two types of cable (pipe) were used for crossing the Channel and these were laid by cable ship, authorities once again striving to suppress their real function. Cables were constructed in 4000 feet lengths, and wound onto six huge drums, which were officially termed "conuns" or "conundrums"[16] – but more informally referred to by locals as "cotton reels" (or as "HMS Conundrum"). These were manufactured at Scunthorpe, but assembled at Tilbury docks, launched into the Thames and floated around the coast to be connected to the land cables.

---

16. A diminution of "cone-ended drums".

3. Defence of the Realm – Wartime

PLUTO pipes being assembled at the RH&DR New Romney station

Each drum was 40 feet in diameter, capable of carrying up to 80 miles of pipe, and weighed 1600 tons. Additionally, some of the steel cables were taken to New Romney by rail, and welded together in longer lengths on the platform of the adjoining RH&DR station. Initially these were then taken on to Dungeness by rail, but they proved to be too heavy for the track and were subsequently moved by road instead. Two of the Navy's most powerful tugs – *HMS Buster* and *HMS Marauder* – were used to tow the 16 cables so involved across the Channel.

PLUTO was an audacious project, with Dwight Eisenhower, the Supreme Commander of the Allied Forces in Europe, describing it as being "second in daring only to the artificial Mulberry harbours". But it was also a hugely resource-intensive operation, involving men from the Royal Engineers, the Pioneer Corps, the Royal Army Service Corps and the Military Police. As the oil reached the coast, the operation required a number of pumping stations and other operational buildings to facilitate the next stage of its journey. These also had to be protected from aerial surveillance, so all installations had to be disguised. For the most part, existing buildings were taken over and their roofs removed. Walls were then strengthened and reinforced to protect the pumps and tanks in case of a direct hit by enemy bombs, before the roofs were replaced. At Dungeness, a number of buildings were specially constructed, but designed to resemble bungalows or garages when seen from above. Dungeness hosted a number of PLUTO buildings, which included pumping stations. One would later be used as the headquarters for the local Royal Antediluvian Order of Buffaloes (RAOB) lodge and as a community hall. It even, for a time, served as the local chapel, for which reason it remains known as The Sanctuary.[17]

---

17. It seems that The Sanctuary and its neighbours may well have originally been built to accommodate troops, but were adapted for PLUTO purposes.

Two of the surviving PLUTO buildings, in 2013 (that to the left is The Sanctuary, in the process of being converted)

The secretive and sensitive nature of the PLUTO operation necessitated enhanced access restrictions and, in 1944, Dungeness became officially upgraded from a restricted area to a demarcation zone, with armed sentries posted to the east at Derville Road and on the coast road from Littlestone. Understandably, those residents allowed to remain in the area were sworn to secrecy as to what might be going on.

By necessity, in places the wartime PLUTO pipeline passed close to the fishermen's houses in the north of Dungeness village. Ken Oiller recalls[18] an evening when an army officer raced round, banging on doors to warn that the pipe had been damaged and was spurting petrol. Luckily no naked lights/fires were burning, but a more lasting legacy was that the petrol had seeped into the water course, contaminating local supplies. In the short-term, the military established bowsers from which the residents could collect supplies but, soon after, a permanent water supply was installed to all cottages at Dungeness.

The technology involved in PLUTO was undoubtedly excellent, and represented a remarkable feat of engineering, but the results were not outstanding. The pipeline from Walton-on-Thames to the coast had been completed by the end of 1943, but the laying of sea cables[19] did not begin until October 1944. The reasons for this delay were two-fold: first, the Boulogne approaches had to be cleared of mines; then, extreme bad weather resulted in the cable ships having to leave the Channel to seek shelter. So, by the second week in December, only six of the 16 cables had been laid. Although, once installed, the pipework was used daily until the end of June 1945, only 700 tons of petrol crossed the channel each day by these means – less than 8% of all required oil products.

Other new technology

PLUTO was not the only piece of new technology to come out of WWII. Being at the forefront of Britain's defences and relatively unoccupied, the area was quite often used for experimentation and testing purposes and, accordingly, attracted some high-profile interest. In 1944,

---

18. *Dungeness Remembered*.
19. The first cable-laying ship was originally named *Empire Baffin* but, following conversion, was renamed *HMS Sandycroft*. It is believed that this was after Asquith's residence at nearby Littlestone, but corroboration is lacking.

rumours began to circulate that a familiar figure had graced Dungeness with his presence. Such was the closed nature of communications that it was not until some time later that it was confirmed that prime minister, Winston Churchill, had visited. In fact, he was just one of a number of Allied leaders who had gathered at the Hope & Anchor pub at Pen Bars to watch experiments involving a new, state-of-the-art flamethrower.[20]

Incidents and Casualties

Inevitably, the strategic importance of both the Dover Straits and the Kent skies (as the Battle of Britain raged) meant that Dungeness saw far more than its fair share of conflict and loss of life. But battle in the skies did not start overnight. In his book *Romney Marsh at War*, Ted Carpenter quotes fisherman Ben Tart, a member of the ROC, as saying: "after war was declared it remained quiet. We wondered what it was all about. Occasionally Jerry would send over a plane or two, just to let you know he was still there". Early damage was self-inflicted rather than the result of enemy action, as previously described. Apart from the near destruction of the lifeboat house, the first real incident of note occurred on 7 October 1939 when a mine, which had earlier washed ashore at Dengemarsh, detonated. Although nobody was hurt, a coastguard lookout was wrecked. From then on, exploding naval mines became a fairly regular phenomenon at Dungeness, but with damage still restricted to property. In the following month, a number of bodies, believed to be those of a German U-boat crew, washed ashore at Dungeness.

Moving into 1940, Admiralty mines that had broken free of their wires continued to cause problems and, after a Folkestone vessel had been blown to pieces with all four crew being killed, the Dungeness fishermen asked the Admiralty to reconsider its practices. This request met with silence and, shortly after (in March), another string of mines broke loose in strong winds. As a consequence, fishermen were unable to go to sea for nearly a month. At sea, the first major conflict of note was in June 1940, when the steamship *MV Roseburn* was torpedoed by two German E-boats[21] off Dungeness Point. Members of the ROC had apparently noticed the two fast-moving vessels and called HQ. But there had been no previous E-boat activity in the area, and HQ assumed that the men had been mistaken – so the report was not acted upon. The *Roseburn* was beached and remained undisturbed until after the war, when – deemed to be a danger to shipping and fishermen – it was blown up.

From the skies, the first documented incident was a damaged Spitfire, which crash-landed near the water tower between Lydd and Dungeness in June 1940. Increasingly, German bombers that had not dropped their load on strategic targets would empty their chambers before returning across the channel – meaning that Dungeness sometimes became the default target. Although no serious injury resulted, there was again some damage to property, particularly windows.

---

20. It has also been reported (post war) that Churchill made an earlier visit with General Pile (to inspect the wider coastal defences).
21. Fast torpedo launches.

The MV Roseburn, *beached at Dungeness, on 20 June 1940*

The Battle of Britain officially started on 10 July 1940 and, on that day, following an aerial skirmish, three planes crashed into the sea off Lade and a fourth – a German Dornier – came down near the Dungeness Buoy. A week later, two Hurricanes on escort duty were separated from their colleagues when attacked by a force of more than 20 enemy aircraft. One of these, with Pilot Office Vic Ortmans at the controls, was hit, but managed to make a forced landing on the beach at Dengemarsh, from where his plane was successfully recovered. Later the same month, troops at the Dengemarsh searchlight battery were machine-gunned by a German fighter plane, but avoided injury. From then on, until the end of the Battle of Britain on 31 October 1940, a number of both allied and German planes came down on the Dungeness or Dengemarsh beaches, or crashed into the sea nearby. One such incident (in September) was witnessed by John and Bob Oiller, who were fishing off Dungeness Point. The plane had crashed into the sea in flames, but the Oillers saw that the pilot had parachuted out shortly before. They were able to recover him from the water, and land him safely at Galloways.

That the dangers posed by poor protocols had not receded was underlined when a soldier from the Somerset Light Infantry was killed after stepping on a landmine at Dungeness in September of the same year. But attention reverted to the skies a few months later when, on 16 April 1941, Pilot Officers Boguslaw Mierzwa and Mieczyslaw Waskiewicz from 303 Polish Squadron, RAF Northolt, were returning from escorting six Bristol Blenheim light bombers on a mission in France. Intercepted and attacked over the Channel, Mierzwa's Spitfire came down in flames close to the school; Waskiewicz's plane crashed into the sea nearby, but neither this nor the bodies of the two pilots were ever found.

Local children placed a small but poignant tribute to Mierzwa outside the school, but there have been two further memorials to the Polish airmen. The site of both has been the shingle between the RH&DR station and the former RNSSS cottages. The first was placed by Greatstone resident Colin Clayton, with the pole holding the flag fashioned from a piece of

3. Defence of the Realm – Wartime

Pilot Officer Vic Ortman's Hurricane, which had made a forced landing at Dengemarsh on 17 July 1940, being recovered by crane

redundant RH&DR rail. This was replaced in April 2016 (the 75th anniversary of the deaths) by a more substantial structure and wooden bench, funded and erected by the owners of the power station (EDF Energy) and Polish members of its workforce.

This was not the full extent of the 1941 casualties, and two enemy craft crashed on the same June day – one near the water tower on Denge Beach, the other at Dengemarsh. By this time, the sight of British and German aircraft flying erratically after suffering serious damage

The original memorial to Boguslaw Mierzwa and Mieczyslaw Waskiewicz (left) and its replacement, which has been described as one of the simplest, yet most moving war memorials in Britain

had become a regular occurrence. In November, a German commercial aircraft that had been stolen by two young Frenchmen seeking to join the Free French forces, crash-landed near the Britannia pub. The men were fortunate in that they were flying an unknown plane, yet had not attracted ack-ack fire. A relatively quieter couple of years followed, with fewer incidents recorded in, off or above Dungeness in 1942. Whilst the Prebble family was finally forced to vacate their Dengemarsh home for good,[22] this was as much due to the danger from practice firing on the Lydd ranges as to the threat posed by German bombs. In November 1943, a German Junkers 88 aircraft was shot down just off Dungeness Point with the loss of all three crew, and the following month a British Hurricane crashed onto the beach after its pilot had ejected. Prior to this, at the start of May 1943, the tiny remaining Dungeness community had raised the astonishing sum of £2825 towards the cost of a new Spitfire, as part of the Wings for Victory Week.

Residents also reported witnessing a German Junkers 88 bomber trailing a white scarf from the window crash-landing in front of the Britannia, with the crew immediately surrendering; and Ken Oiller additionally recalled an American bomber crashing just to the south east of Pen Bars. The only casualty apparently sustained by its crew was a broken leg, suffered in a misjudged attempt to leap clear from the top of the cockpit. Although not possible to date these events with absolute certainty, it seems likely that both would have been in 1943. More certainly datable to that year was another near "own goal" which occurred on the 25 November, when a returning British aircraft unloaded nine incendiary bombs on to the beach near the Dungeness border. It was reported to have been a bright, moonlit night, but clearly not bright enough, as The Pilot Inn was very nearly annihilated. Two months later, on the night of 21–22 January 1944, a Dornier aircraft shot down by Mosquito pilots crashed into the sea just south of Dungeness.

On 24 April 1944, the American B17 Flying Fortress bomber, *Sleepytime Girl*, was returning from a daytime bombing raid on a German aircraft factory when it suffered heavy flak

The Dungeness portion of the £10,000 Wings for Victory target was £2000, which was comfortably exceeded

---

22. From 1940 they had been required to leave their home during daylight hours due to the risks posed by practice shelling.

3. Defence of the Realm – Wartime

Sleepytime Girl *in flying condition (left), and one of its engines, as recovered from the ocean after 73 years*

damage. All four engines cut out, but, by diving to 5,000 feet, the pilot managed to restart them. The crew then had to decide whether to head for Switzerland or try to make it back to Britain. They opted for the latter, which, with the benefit of hindsight, was probably the wrong choice: because of the low altitude at which it was forced to fly, the plane was wide open to further attack and now enemy aircraft completely destroyed three of the engines. Despite this, and with six of the ten crew either dead or dying, those remaining very nearly managed to limp back over the Channel on the one working engine. Forced to ditch the plane off just off Dungeness Point, the crew members who had survived were, fortunately, picked up by an amphibious biplane.

The tragic loss of six crew members might have formed just another footnote in history, but for local fisherman Joe Thomas, some 73 years later. Thomas was fishing in the area when his nets snagged on an unidentified heavy object. When he managed – after two days – to get this to the surface, it turned out to be one of the one-ton radial engines of *Sleepytime Girl*, with the three propeller blades surprisingly still intact. The engine was cleaned and mounted and is now on display in the garden of The Pilot Inn, a memorial to those brave young men who perished fighting for the allied cause.

1944 would prove to be a major turning point in the war, as what would become known as D-Day (6 June) approached. In preparation for this, some of the spare Phoenix caissons – the building blocks for the celebrated Mulberry harbour – were stored in the east bay, off Dungeness. There were concerns that these might be targeted by German bombers, but this threat never materialised. Activity in the Channel at this time did become frenzied, though, and E-boats were responsible for sinking two ships in a convoy off the Point. Soon after, on 22 June, another incident took place that again involved an American bomber. An USAAF raid on the railway line at Tournan-en-Brie had been unsuccessful, in that it had been imprecise and resulted in the deaths of a number of civilians. Perhaps because of this, the bombers were pursued with particular intensity, and attacked. One was severely damaged, but just managed to clear the Channel before crash landing on Dungeness Beach.

Doodlebugs

Also in June 1944, as the war entered its final stages, the Germans tried one final throw of the dice. This was in the form of V1 flying bombs. These doodlebugs, as they became more familiarly known,[23] were launched from mobile ramps in Pas de Calais and Picardy, and were generally targeted on London – thus entering UK airspace between Hythe and Dungeness.

Some days, there would be in excess of 30 of these doodlebugs crossing the Channel, in batches of up to five or even six at a time. Records are quite contradictory, but some sources suggest that there may have been in excess of 1000 bombs entering English airspace in the 80 days or so that they were deployed. The sinister nature of the weapon, flown low over the water and posing a direct threat only when the engines had cut out and the noise had stopped, meant that they were most feared and remembered by those who endured the war. Despite this, however, fatalities were relatively slight. When spotted from the Dungeness Observer Corps tower, a parachute flare would be fired to alert the army gun emplacements, and anti-aircraft gunfire would frequently light up the sky in response. A number of doodlebugs were downed on and around Dungeness and Dengemarsh, and still more crashed into the sea. But there was frustration arising from the fact that the Dungeness ROC post was armed mainly only with Bofors guns, which were not powerful enough to do much more than dent the missiles. In reality, the main defence against the flying bombs was the American 125th Anti-Aircraft Gun Battalion based nearby at Littlestone – right in the middle of the flightpath.

Capture of Spies

Hitler's plans to invade centred on the landing of troops from the 17th and 35th Divisions of the XIII Corps of the 16th Army, at a point between Folkestone and Dungeness. Clearly, these plans were ultimately unrealised, but there were spies who did successfully make the journey. Just how many reached these shores is open to debate, but it is known that four members of the Abwehr, the German military intelligence service, made it across the Channel in September 1940. Their mission was simply to carry out surveillance in advance of the intended invasion. The four crossed the Channel by fishing boat but, when a few hundred yards from land, transferred to rowing boats. Two landed at Hythe, whilst the others – Karl Heinrich Meier (a Dutchman of German origin) and Jose Waldberg – beached at Dungeness.

To say that this was not the most carefully planned and executed wartime escapade would be a gross understatement. From start to finish, it was a catalogue of disasters. Even the spy-

---

23. Other names regularly used to describe this weapon included "Diver" (a code name) and "buzz-bomb".

masters were so aware of its limited chances of success that they informally referred to the plan as the *Himmelfahrt* (the ascension to heaven). None of the participants displayed any real aptitude for spying, and the equipment that they brought with them was demonstrably unsuited to the task. For Meier and Waldberg, things started to go wrong even before they landed. Incorrectly believing that they had been spotted, they ditched most of their provisions and maps overboard whilst at sea. On landing, they hid what remained of their food and drink under the beached boat and, carrying the small radio transmitters they had brought with them, moved inland. They camped close to the Dungeness Road but, the next morning, when hungry and thirsty, decided it was too risky to return to their reserves on the beach. Instead, Meier – the only one of the party who could speak English and who had any experience of living in the UK – undertook to search out the area. On reaching Lydd, he entered the Rising Sun public house where his accent and lack of awareness of English protocols immediately aroused suspicion. He was soon arrested and led the police to Waldberg at their makeshift camp. Here, the police also discovered the crude transmitter which would ultimately determine their fate. Both Meier and Waldberg were later hanged at Pentonville Prison, under the newly-introduced Treachery Act.

Legacy

There are plenty of reminders of WWII – and of post-war military use – still to be found in the area. At various locations, concrete debris gives clues to the site of a gun emplacement or defensive structure. From time to time, too, sections of the PLUTO pipeline, doodlebug remnants or even parts of downed aircraft are uncovered by the action of a high tide. But

17 years after the incident, and after his own retirement from the force, former Sgt Tye points rather self-consciously to the holly bush on the Dungeness Road where the spies first hid and transmitted messages

perhaps the most dramatic and obvious signs are the craters which remain, particularly to the west (on Denge Beach and at Pen Bars). These are not necessarily the result of enemy action: most bear witness to the fact that parts of the beach were used as target areas for shelling practice during the war. The majority of these craters are the result of firing from as far away as Ham Street and Orlestone Wood, as well as more locally from Lydd. Others resulted from the post-war exercise to clear land and anti-tank mines (which in some cases also resulted in the death of pets and domestic animals – as referenced elsewhere).

Impact of the Ranges

Although the threat of invasion has clearly receded, the Lydd Ranges – established over 150 years ago – continue to be used for military training purposes and, having been extended eastward over the years, now border Dengemarsh. The risks posed by live firing are not confined to the ranges, however, as shells can travel several miles out to sea – so there is a need to monitor compliance with the coastal exclusion zone when exercises are under way. The former Dengemarsh coastguard lookout is one of a number now used for monitoring this compliance, but it is not the first building here to have served the purpose. The need to provide better sightlines to sea was first recognised in the 1920s and, in this decade, a discrete army lookout was constructed on the beach. This was of very distinctive design, and mirrored that of another tower just to the west, at Galloways. Both were generally manned by civilian staff, and both were demolished in 1968.

The unusual Army lookout tower at Dengemarsh, pictured shortly before demolition in 1968. Note the extant coastguard lookout tower just behind (Photo courtesy Ted Carpenter)

4

War on Smuggling – Revenue Protection

The same physical attributes that made the coastline of Dungeness and the wider Romney Marsh vulnerable to invasion have also made the area very attractive to "freetraders", or smugglers. The absence of prying eyes, and the closeness of the community, have been additional factors in protecting them.

Although smuggling – a consequence of taxation – can be traced back to the tenth century, concerted measures to combat it didn't really come about until 700 years later. Even then, arrangements were often hopelessly inefficient. The incidence of smuggling at Dungeness up until this time (and even beyond) is difficult to determine, although there was a building known as Bangtails somewhere near the site of Dungeness A power station,[1] which was generally believed to have been the centre of the free trade here. There are anecdotal accounts of many smuggling enterprises, as well as of the darker practice of wrecking. This, of course, is true of many coastal communities. In reality, historical records suggest that most of the significant smuggling activity in the area was probably organised from Lydd.

Counter-smuggling arrangements

As related in earlier chapters, bodies answerable for national defence have at different times also taken on some responsibility for counter-smuggling activities. The Coastguard Service – which is now focused on lifesaving, with some additional coastal observation duties – once took the lead role in the fight against smuggling, but was itself the result of reorganisation of other bodies. By the 17th century, the Board of Customs operated a small fleet of boats, which could be backed by resources from the Royal Navy – but their numbers precluded anything other than spasmodic patrols. Ashore, the Customs Officers could call upon units of local dragoons, although these were hopelessly under-manned. But, in 1698, the Treasury and Board of Customs established a contingent of Riding Officers in Kent and Sussex to help combat the increasing loss of revenue resulting from the "free trade". By the early 18th century, this force had expanded to around 300 men. Meanwhile, back at sea, the small fleet of Revenue sloops struggled to tackle effectively the bigger and better armed smuggling vessels. However, Warren Lisle, Surveyor of Sloops of the South

---

1. An area then known locally as Brick House Point.

Coast,[2] managed to procure new, larger and better armed vessels for the purpose. By 1782, there were in service some 40 new vessels, which carried 700 crewmen and could deploy 200 guns. This marked a significant change in the balance of power between the smugglers and the government and, in 1809, arrangements were further refined with the creation of the Preventive Water Guard (PWG). This introduced dedicated preventive boats (usually rowing boats crewed by staff based in Watch Houses), which patrolled the shallow waters of their defined stretch of coast each night, picking off those smugglers who had managed to get past the cutters. The PWG became part of a three-pronged approach, complementing not just the work of the preventive cruiser crews, but also that of the shore-based Riding Officers. It operated under the centralised control of Customs and, although its primary role was prevention of smuggling, it also had some responsibility for life saving in the event of a shipwreck.

In a single week in 1813, smugglers landed an astonishing 12,000 gallons of brandy on Dungeness Beach. Yet it was still reported that the end of the Napoleonic Wars, two years later, resulted in a huge upsurge in smuggling activity in the area. This was no coincidence; the French conflict had resulted in crippling poverty for many and the agricultural workers in Kent and Sussex were amongst the most poorly fed, housed and paid. For them, smuggling was not just a means of improving quality of life, it was often crucial for the survival of their families. In a bid to counter the growth of the free trade, Captain Joseph McCulloch – commander of a Royal Naval ship tasked with supporting the Revenue Service – proposed the creation of a unified service to guard the Kent coast, run along naval lines. His suggestion was that the three lines of defence should be brigaded under a single command. This was largely implemented with the creation of the Coast Blockade Service (CBS)[3] in 1816. It was run by McCulloch himself, reporting to the Treasury, and operated between Dungeness and North Foreland. Although the service did have some notable successes, it was extremely costly and did not totally eradicate the duplication and role confusion of previous arrangements. Furthermore, McCulloch had a reputation as a fierce disciplinarian. Unpopular with his men, he made liberal use of the cat o'nine tails[4] and, as a result, morale was often poor. Accordingly, his men were not always keen to fight and, like some of the Riding Officers, sometimes open to the taking of a bribe.

As recounted in Chapter 3, the RN Shore Signal Stations had been closed in 1814 when the Napoleonic threat had receded. Their potential for use in the fight against smuggling, however, was recognised and, in 1818, many stations – including that at Dungeness – were re-opened as the Admiralty set up a system to cover the coast between Beachy Head and Deal. At this time, the Popham semaphore system had just been developed to replace the old shut-

---

2. Between 1740 and 1779.
3. The Royal Naval Coastal Blockade Service for the Prevention of Smuggling, to give its full title.
4. Giving rise to his nickname: *Flogging Joey*.

4. War on Smuggling – Revenue Protection

The RNSSS cottages on the old redoubt site (2018), which are now owned by EDF and leased out. It is unlikely that these are the same buildings erected in 1820, although it has not been possible to prove otherwise (see Chapter 3)

ter technology and this greatly improved communications between blockade stations and revenue cutters. The semaphore comprised a tall mast with two arms attached to chains, operated by naval staff from within a wooden shed at the base. As a result of teething problems and the enormity of the conversion work, the system did not become operational until 1820, but line drawings from the period showing these arms demonstrate that, from the outset, the re-vamped Dungeness Signal Station also operated from within the redoubt. Dedicated RNSSS cottage accommodation was constructed on the site for staff.

The Dungeness preventive boat was one of a fleet of ten, each crewed by a chief officer, a sitter (coxswain) and between six and eight boatmen. It undertook patrols at night, whilst maintaining a token watch during daylight hours. In terms of the location of the blockade station, there are once again contradictions within source material. Some records state that it was based at No. 2 Battery – i.e. at Lade. This would seem unlikely, given the location of the RN Signal Station and it is more probable that it would have been at the No. 1 battery site.

In terms of shore patrols (the Riding Officer function) – the third element of McCulloch's strategy – precise details of activity at Dungeness at this time are typically unclear. Maps of 1818 show a customs building that was presumably a warehouse for storage of seized contraband, which does suggest the presence of Riding Officers.[5] There are also references to Coastguard officers being based here very soon after the formal establishment of the service

---

5. At about this time, a raid was undertaken on the building by smugglers, although this appears to have been led by a gang comprising inhabitants of The Brooks, Lydd and Jury's Gap rather than by (the obviously more law abiding!) residents of Dungeness itself. Much of the smuggling on this part of the coast continued to be organised and controlled by gangs from Lydd and further afield.

The derelict shack on the fishing beach known locally as the Customs Building (in quite obvious need of some tender, loving care) in 2018. This is not on the same site as the building of that name shown on the 1818 map (and it is almost certain that this stretch of beach would have been beneath the sea at this time)

in 1822, and it seems that at least one ancestor of a Dungeness fishing family (the Richardsons) may have first come to the area to take up duties as a coastguard.

Later Developments

In 1821, a wider review of revenue protection services recommended that they should all be brigaded under the Board of Customs, with the exception of the Coast Blockade, which would remain under the control of the Admiralty. This resulted in the creation of a new Coast Guard Service in 1822. In 1831, the Coast Blockade, too, was formally absorbed into this new service. At the same time, the Admiralty determined that the Coast Guard Service should additionally act as a reserve force for the Royal Navy.

From the 1830s, events are better recorded and less open to dispute. One of the less obvious consequences of the many administrative changes is reflected in correspondence sent to the Dungeness Coast Guard by senior management. Whereas the Coast Blockade Service had used contractors to supply fresh water in barrels, which were rolled over the shingle, the Coast Guard now favoured donkeys to undertake the transport duties. But the cost savings were not evident and the local coastguards were accused of keeping the animals "at levels of extravagance". They were instructed to stop buying beans for their donkeys and to cut down on the quantities of oats being fed to them!

From 1840, the UK government's decision to abandon mercantilism, and adopt free trade policies, had a significant impact on smuggling activity. Tobacco now took over from alcohol as the most lucrative commodity to be imported illegally in any quantity, and more imaginative techniques were used to bring it into the country. Although this must have still been of concern to the authorities, with the volume of commercial shipping increasing at a great rate they

4. War on Smuggling – Revenue Protection

For many years, donkeys remained in favour with the Coastguard Service for the collection of provisions, particularly at remote stations. Pictured is a young member of the Spry family from No. 3 Coastguard Station at Denge, c. 1912. Note also that he is wearing backstays

now channelled their resources more towards vessels and individuals in danger, and to protecting shipwrecks from looters. The number of cruisers patrolling the waters was reduced and, from 1849, the Riding Officer role effectively disappeared. In 1856, at the end of the Crimean War, another political reorganisation found the whole Coast Guard Service back under the control of the Admiralty.

Whilst, from this time onwards, there is little firm evidence of large-scale smuggling at Dungeness, the battle had by no means been won. There were still cargoes of alcohol, as well as tobacco being landed illegally, and fishermen were not averse to using their boats for such a purpose. Many pubs on the Marsh were still actively involved (providing a ready market for contraband) and the isolated nature of the Hope & Anchor at Pen Bars made its own role in the activity inevitable. There is evidence of fines being handed down to its landlords, even as

The Hope & Anchor, c. 1928

late as the 1940s, when its incumbent was prosecuted after a customs officer found small quantities of tobacco secreted on the premises. Acting on a tip-off, he undertook a thorough search, which included the contents of pans boiling on the stove. Although finding a few pouches hidden behind some pictures hanging on the wall, he failed to find the main "stash".

Current Day

The goods of value have continued to change over time, with drugs and people now being more attractive commodities than alcohol and tobacco. Smuggling today tends to be a much more sophisticated affair, and carrying an illicit cargo across the Channel in small boats – given the intense monitoring of its busy shipping lanes – is not an attractive risk to the serious free-trader. Any large cargoes are now more likely to be brought into the country by ferry or by air.

The very nature of smuggling makes it difficult to quantify the extent of the problem, and official figures can only be rough estimates. When the market for recreational drugs first developed, official sources denied that there was a problem at Dungeness, but locals will tell you of having regularly found "mystery" packages on the beach, dropped by light aircraft that had crossed the Channel. Similarly, the same residents will, if pressed, divulge the names of individuals that they are sure were regularly bringing illegal immigrants into the country as long ago as the 1970s.

Smuggling has traditionally thrived when people have been desperate, and prepared to take risks that most would see as unattractive. Notable within this category are refugees now fleeing poverty and genocide, and prepared to risk all to get to the UK. Willing to spend disproportionate amounts of money to achieve this goal, they fall prey to owners of boats that are often unsuited to the task. By way of illustration (and following rumours of numerous refugees having turned up at Dungeness over the previous months), in May 2016, 16 Albanian immigrants together with two UK people smugglers were rescued in the Channel by the Dungeness lifeboat, having nearly capsized in their totally inadequate inflatable. In January 2018, the same lifeboat saved the lives of a further nine Albanian refugees (including a woman and two children) off the same coast.

This politically motivated addition to the estate management sign was one of a number to appear in 2018. The sticker was the reflection of an individual's cynicism rather than the stance of EDF!

5

Saving the Mariner – Coastguard and Lifeboat Services

The Coastguard Service

Nowadays, we associate the governmental (as opposed to RNLI or lifeguard) role of coastal search and rescue with the Coastguard Service – part of the Maritime & Coastguard Agency (MCA). But, as detailed in the previous chapter, it was only from 1856 that the Coastguard Service lost its counter-smuggling role and started to morph into an organisation that we would recognise today. As already discussed, many of the officers recruited from this time were those who would otherwise have served (or continued to serve) in the Royal Navy, but were unable to do so for reasons of age or ill-health.

The new Coast Guard Service (as it was then called) initially made use of existing staff accommodation inherited from blockade days and from other bodies, but later (between 1878 and 1905) invested heavily in a building programme of its own. Cottages were built to a robust standard, and many survive today – sometimes on the site of earlier blockade buildings. To recap, at Dungeness, they were at the entrance to the estate and are now officially known

Dengemarsh Coastguard officers, 1895

The Denge Coastguard cottage, at the entrance to the Dungeness estate, with part of the original Watch House to the rear left (see also Chapter 3)

as the Denge (sometimes Dunge) Coastguard cottages. They were built in 1878, probably replacing some earlier and more basic Coastguard accommodation on the same site.

An ancillary building which, unfortunately, has not stood the test of time, was the Earth House. This was built[1] for Coastguard officers and their families: in the days prior to indoor sanitation, earth closets were seen as providing a degree of luxury and privacy. Because of the geology, supplies of earth had to be delivered by cart from Lydd, and stored in a purpose-built shed (the Earth House). The Coastguard cottage residents would supposedly collect earth and lime from here by pail, and take it back home (to throw over excrement). In the event, many residents found the Earth House to be too far away to be practicable – particularly in bad weather – and, like the fishing families, chose instead to dispose of their waste straight onto the beach.

The Earth House was located near the entrance to the estate. It is believed that this may have been the last surviving example of its kind in the country, but was unfortunately demolished at the end of the 1970s, soon after this picture was taken

1. Another GH Bates of Lydd construction.

Lifesaving companies and rocket launchers

For incidents closer to the shore, or in the event of a wrecked vessel, an important part of the rescuers' armoury in the late 19th century was the breeches buoy. This was a crude rope-based flotation device with a leg harness attached. Deployed sometimes by kite system or Lyle gun, in most cases it was a rocket that was used to attach a line to the stricken vessel (either ship to ship or shore to ship). The person being rescued would then be pulled to shore in the breeches buoy, riding the line in much the same way as a zip wire. Life-saving Rocket Companies were formed, which comprised volunteers assisting the Coastguards – although membership was far from mutually exclusive. Each of the Coastguard stations around the Romney Marsh coastline had its own lifesaving crew, and one of the more prominent of these was the Lydd Lifesaving Company, which was formed in 1864 and operated at the Brooks. In 1891, it moved to Dungeness.

Maps of various vintages record rocket posts (with associated rocket stores) located on different sites around the 'Ness, each of which was the responsibility of the Lydd Company. These posts, in part, mirrored the movement of the lifeboat stations. In reality, they were only rarely used in anger, and the abiding memory of older 'Nessers is of the peace being shattered every Thursday morning at 10 o'clock, when routine rocket testing took place.

Into the 20th century

Signal Station/Coastguard Lookouts

Whilst the earlier reorganisations had helped to clarify coast watching responsibilities, there were still some grey areas, coupled with a lack of logic when viewed from the distance of time. The Signal Stations (although now more commonly referred to as Lookouts) continued to operate under the control of the Admiralty, but, at Dungeness, the further build-up of shingle – and possibly also the interruption of sight lines when the new (1904) lighthouse was built – necessitated a change of location. The new site was just to the south of the lighthouse, and the building opened in 1905.

Between 1923 and 1925, the Royal Naval Shore Signal Station designation was officially re-instated, and yet another reconfiguration of responsibilities took place. In recognition of the skills acquired when its members were manning signal stations under Admiralty command, provision was also made at this time for the use of new safety-at-sea communication technologies. There was a renewed initiative to recruit and train rescue volunteers, which would lead to the establishment of the Coastal Life-saving Corps – although this did not become formally established until 1931.[2] This reorganisation further meant that "certain of the duties hitherto performed by (His) Majesty's Coastguard under the Board of Admiralty (were now)

---

2. This would subsequently be re-named the Coastguard Auxiliary Service.

carried out by employees of the Board of Trade and Board of Customs at all Stations other than certain Admiralty Shore Signal Stations where the duties are performed by the Admiralty on behalf of the Board of Trade".[3] The exceptions were those stations that were deemed to have strategic defence importance and they included Dungeness. The Dungeness tower would also become an important look-out facility in WWII.

The Shore Signal Station network officially survived into the early 1950s, when those stations remaining under Admiralty control were, finally, transferred to HM Coastguard. Once again, however, Dungeness, was atypical. The building here, as the 1904 lighthouse, was becoming increasingly further from the sea as a result of the relentless action of longshore drift. It was also starting to show its age. HM Coastguard now introduced a new network of radar monitoring stations to observe shipping in the channel and, whilst mainly using existing signal station infrastructure to meet its needs, decided that the Dungeness building was unsuitable.[4] Accordingly, the lookout facility at nearby Lade was chosen to serve this part of the coast.

Yet another reappraisal of strategy resulted in a new lookout tower being constructed at Dungeness, which in turn signalled the end for the Lade Coastguard. Many sources relate that

The Dungeness Shore Signals Station (left) c. 1940, manned by the Admiralty. From this time, photographs show a proliferation of aerials (and later radar masts) on the Ness: these were erected not only by the Admiralty, but also by Trinity House (for directional wireless) and the Decca research company

3. From the *London Gazette*, 6 May 1925.
4. This was seemingly demolished in the late 1940s.

5. Saving the Mariner – Coastguard and Lifeboat Services

this was built in 1950,[5] but these are incorrect. In the absence of official records, there debate continues as to when the new lookout was actually constructed. Built by Terry & Carpenter, it is shown in a photograph purporting to date from 1976, but there is no corroborating evidence of it existing at this time. Numerous residents recall it being there in the late 1970s, which is probably when it was first used. Regardless of any debate over dates, the new tower was initially manned by Coastguard staff still living at Lade. Although this new lookout was constructed to accommodate a radar scanner, it was subsequently decided to approach the power station for permission to mount that on the top of one of the reactor towers – because of the latter's greater elevation. This was all well and good until the hurricane of 1987, when it was blown off its mounting. A nuclear inspector, surveying the damage to the power station caused by the hurricane, spotted the displaced scanner and determined that it had to go.

At this time, the Dungeness Coastguard was responsible for the whole stretch of coast between the River Rother and the Hythe redoubt. The new lookout served until the late 1980s, before further strategic and technological changes resulted in it becoming largely obsolete. Many of the functions were now being undertaken regionally, from Dover, although initial concerns over resilience meant that the Dungeness building was retained for operational reasons in the short term. It was also occasionally used in bad weather and for training purposes, so was not formally decommissioned until 1997. The following year, it was privately purchased for £35,000 by a couple who spent a further £75,000 and two years of their time converting it into a four-storey residential property with two balconies and a terrace. It is now let out as a rather distinctive holiday home.

The picture on the left is believed to be of Dungeness Coastguard lookout shortly after completion (photo courtesy Ted Carpenter); the lookout is shown (right) after enhancement and subsequent conversion to holiday accommodation

---

5. Probably reflecting that the previous Dungeness lookout had been decommissioned a few years earlier.

Nanny Goat Island

Denge Marsh Lookout (Pen Bars)

In the war years, Coastguard staff (reporting to officers at Lade) had occupied the Dengemarsh army lookout[6] at night. Post-war, they were granted continued access rights, which lasted up until 1960, when a dedicated Coastguard lookout was constructed on the western part of the 'Ness, close to the outfall. This never became a key part of Coastguard strategy, and was mainly used by Auxiliaries in rough weather, before in turn being sold off to the MoD.

The Dengemarsh lookout (left) pictured under construction in 1960 (photo courtesy Ted Carpenter); and in 2017, under MOD ownership (note the red flag flying to denote that firing is taking place on the Ranges)

Lifesaving Company changes

In 1938, the Lydd Lifesaving Company moved once more, this time nearer to Galloways and its original base. In 1964, reflecting other rationalisations, it merged with the Lade Group and became the Coast Rescue Company. By this time, rocket apparatus was stored more centrally, being transported by lorry to wherever it was required along the coast. As with the RNLI, there was a great reliance on the public spiritedness of local men to man the Lifesaving Companies, and some served for many years. In this regard, the service of Steve Prebble (who chalked up 54 years of loyal service) was most notable.

Current day

Further rationalisation and administration changes have continued to transform the work and composition of the Coastguard Service. Local teams comprising volunteer Coastguard Rescue

---

6. As described in Chapter 3.

5. Saving the Mariner – Coastguard and Lifeboat Services

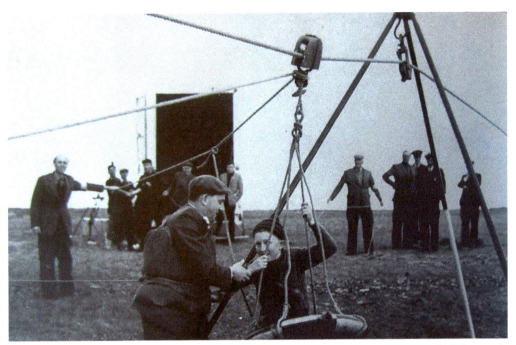

Lydd Lifesaving Company practicing the use of breeches buoy at Galloways, 1962 (photo courtesy Ted Carpenter)

Officers (CROs) now operate under fairly remote management, and the Dungeness Coastguard Rescue Service is one of some 350 teams around the coast. As with many local stations, it is located on an industrial estate. Surprisingly, this is some six miles from Dungeness Point, in Mountfield Road, New Romney.

Sign of the times: rocket posts and traditional Coastguard stations have disappeared, and the MCA's Dungeness' fixed presence is now restricted to this industrial unit at New Romney (2018)

Dungeness Lifeboat services

The Dungeness RNLI Lifeboat Station now guards the English Channel from Folkestone to Rye Bay but, yet again, earlier responsibilities and arrangements were not always clear-cut. Official records, for example, do not always make an obvious distinction between stations located at Dungeness, Littlestone and even St Mary's Bay.

Early lifeboat cover

The first recorded lifeboat to serve this part of the Channel was at Rye, in 1803.[7] This boat, however, served largely only the western side of Dungeness Point. It was not until 1826 that shipping in the east bay was more formally served, with the opening of a station at St Mary's Bay. This was colloquially – and confusingly – widely referred to as Dungeness Station.[8] A new vessel came on to the same station ten years later, but in 1837 was badly damaged attending a stricken collier and had to be sent to London for repair. In the absence of an available replacement, the station was then closed.

This meant that, for the next 16 years, rescues in the east road of Dungeness were once more undertaken by a combination of coastguards and fishermen. This was far from an ideal situation, but one not unusual on many parts of the coast at the time. Unfortunately, during this period, many lives were lost – including those of 19 coastguards in unsuccessful rescue attempts. Understandably, as a result, there were many calls for more satisfactory arrangements to be instigated. But it took two further tragedies – both in 1852 – for these pleas to be heeded.

The first of these incidents occurred in April, when a barque grounded off Dungeness, near the No. 1 Battery (Battery Road). Seven coastguards from the nearby Denge Coastguard station set off to assist, but their boat capsized and four coastguards, as well as two of the crew who had been rescued, died. In December the same year, the *Louise & Emile*, a German brig, was driven ashore at Dengemarsh. The locals assisted Coastguard officers in attempts to effect a rescue in dreadful weather and freezing cold conditions. Whilst at one point they managed to secure a lifeline, a succession of giant waves resulted in the vessel first breaking up, and then being swamped. In total, 40 lives were lost, but perhaps the most harrowing aspect was that bodies were still being washed ashore many days later.

First Dungeness boats

The upshot was the introduction of a dedicated Dungeness Lifeboat station. This could obviously not happen overnight, and the new facility did not come into effect until 1854. A 25 ft

---

7. This predated the establishment of the National Institution for the Preservation of Lives and Property from Shipwrecks in 1824 (and which became The Royal National Lifeboat Institute [RNLI] in 1854).
8. To add to the confusion, it was officially known as Dymchurch No. 27 tower (reflecting its position by Martello tower No. 27).

boat was placed on service near the Coastguard cottages and a boathouse duly built. The carriage-launched boat, however, was found to be too heavy to be practicable; and launches were delayed because horses or sufficient people could not be found to haul the carriage and its cargo over the shingle. This was not the only problem encountered, with newspaper reports describing that the lifeboat was crewed by volunteers who were undoubtedly eager but who, in many cases (as some of the Coastguard staff), were precluded from serving in the Royal Navy for reasons of age or injury.

Change of station

So another, lighter, lifeboat – the *Brave Robert Sheldon* – was procured, and this arrived on station in January 1857. Fears that this vessel might be too light were confirmed when, returning from attending a call, it overturned in heavy seas. Luckily there were no fatalities but, as a result of this incident, a third lifeboat came to the 'Ness, in 1861. This was named the *Providence*, but concerns remained over launching in bad weather. In addition, delays were being regularly incurred because of the distances that crew and helpers had to travel and, after much debate, later the same year the boat was moved to Littlestone. Strangely, the new station continued to be known by the Dungeness name for the next ten years.

On 22 January 1873, after 12 years with no dedicated Dungeness service, disaster struck. The *Northfleet*, a 951-ton Blackwall frigate, was carrying a human cargo of 342 passengers emigrating to Australia, in addition to the crew and pilot; and was further heavily laden with 580 tons of rail and other equipment required for construction of a railway line. The ship had left Gravesend for Hobart (Tasmania) over a week before, but been plagued by dreadful weather, which had forced the crew to anchor several times in the Channel. On the night in question, it was anchored some five kilometres off Dungeness when rammed by a steamer which then disappeared into the night – despite the cries and pleas for assistance from those

An (unknown) artist's impression of the sinking of the Northfleet, *as seen from Dungeness*

on board the *Northfleet*. Within just 45 minutes, because of the heavy load being carried, it had sunk. Distress flares had been fired, but although there were over 200 other vessels in the east bay at the time, all but three ignored them – mostly in the mistaken belief that they were merely requests for a pilot. At the time there was no colour-coding for rockets and, at the subsequent inquest, it was also identified that many boats would have launched from the beach had it been known that a ship was in peril. Such was the suddenness and unexpected nature of the incident, it had only been only possible to release two of the ship's own lifeboats, and one of these had no oars. Whilst the captain would go down with his ship, his example was not followed by many of the crew: he had to fire his revolver at some of them fighting to get to the lifeboats before the women and children. In the resultant panic, 293 lives were lost to drowning, and just 86 were saved. Of these, only two were children and just two more women (one of whom was the captain's wife). In the aftermath, an inquest identified that the errant steamship was the Spanish *Murillo*.[9]

Return to Dungeness

This was one of the worst-ever disasters in the Channel, and it was as a direct result of this that the Dungeness Lifeboat station was reinstated in 1874.[10] Reflecting – as many RNLI boats – the name of its benefactor, the *David Hullett* was the first to come on to the revived station, and remained in service for 13 years. During this time, it was launched 15 times and was credited with saving 27 lives.

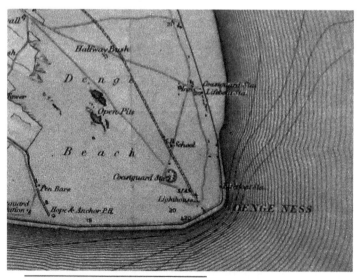

1903 Ordnance Survey map showing the locations of the two lifeboat stations (extract reproduced with kind permission of Ordnance Survey)

9. This was eventually intercepted off Dover some eight months later and its owners compelled to attend a Court of Admiralty. This severely censured her officers and ordered the vessel to be sold by way of penalty.
10. An additional and welcome consequence of this disaster was that a new maritime code was introduced for signalling from sea.

5. Saving the Mariner – Coastguard and Lifeboat Services

A second station

The replacement boat for the *David Hullett*, delivered in 1887, was promoted as the latest in modern technology: a self-righting lifeboat that would also be named after its donor, the *Royal Antediluvian Order of the Buffaloes (RAOB)*. Unfortunately, this didn't live up to its billing, and it capsized twice with loss of crew. The continuing high level of incidents off Dungeness prompted the RNLI to send a much larger self-righting vessel – the *Thomas Simcock* – in 1892.

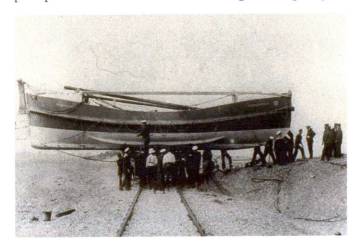

The Thomas Simcox *lifeboat on its carriage (photo courtesy Ted Carpenter)*

Moored in the east bay, nearer to the lighthouse, this did not replace the *RAOB*. The two vessels complemented each other, with the *Thomas Simcox* being officially badged the No. 2 lifeboat. The following year, the *RAOB* was replaced by another self-righting but lighter vessel. This, too, was named the *RAOB* (again being paid for by the Order) and also served alongside its larger counterpart. Soon after (probably in 1895), the *Thomas Simcox* was brought on to the shore (the southern of the two stations shown on the earlier map). It was mounted on a carriage, which in turn ran on a track allowing it to be launched from either the east or south/west beach, depending on sea and wind conditions. This arrangement was found to be no more effective, so a slipway was subsequently built (although there was still no boathouse at this stage).

20th century developments

In 1915, the *Thomas Simcox* was replaced by a new No. 2 boat, the *David Barclay of Tottenham* (a pulling and sailing vessel); and, in 1912, the *Mary Theresa Boileau* took over the role of No. 1 boat from the second *RAOB*. But, in 1939, the rationale for maintaining two boats would be reconsidered, and the No. 1 station closed as a result.

A first motorised lifeboat, the *Charles Cooper Henderson*,[11] replaced the *David Barclay* in 1933, and had a good run – serving until 1957. During these 24 years, it was launched no less than 171 times, saving 63 lives; and, in 1940, was one of 19 RNLI lifeboats that took part in the

---

11. Named after the famous painter of horses and coaches (the donor being a relative).

evacuation of Allied troops from Dunkirk in northern France. Its replacement was the *Mabel E Holland*, a cabin motor lifeboat with twin 48 hp diesel engines. The *Mabel E. Holland* also gave long service, and during its lifetime, what is now known as The Old Boathouse was constructed to accommodate its gear and crew.

This part of the east beach (pictured in 2017) hosted the Dungeness lifeboat between 1921 and 1977. The red and white building (constructed in 1966) was the gear store, whilst the grey shed to the right was the winch house. There is nothing remaining of a lifeboat house here; the hard standing that survives was part of a shed for a bulldozer used to counter the movement of shingle

Another relocation

The relentless impact of longshore drift, however, meant that, by the 1970s, the lifeboat was a significant distance from the sea. The former No. 2 station had already been moved closer to the shore during its lifetime, but this time it was decided to completely re-locate. The preferred site seemed to reflect history: a move back north along the coast. In March 1974, a planning application was submitted to New Romney Town Council for the building of a new boathouse at Littlestone, which was estimated to cost in excess of £100k. Local newspapers carried the headline: "RNLI to move to Littlestone", but it seems that local opposition resulted in the application being withdrawn. Instead, an alternative site was selected at Dungeness – near to The Pilot Inn, and not far from another previous base. The new station was opened in 1977, and cost £45k – a smaller, but still significant, investment. A new lifeboat – the *Alice Upjohn* – was also delivered. This was of the new Rother class of craft, and smaller than the majority of her predecessors.

The new boat was carriage-launched (requiring the use of a tractor) and, at the outset, was still formally under test. There were some problems in re-siting the winch from the old station but, although these were soon addressed, the *Mabel E Holland* was retained in service on the old site until January 1979. The official line was that the two vessels were working in tandem, but the reality was that many had concerns over the latest launching technology and wanted to retain a back-up. In practice, these fears proved unfounded. When the old slipway was finally dismantled, the piles were removed and used in the construction of the car park at the new lifeboat station – where they remain in situ.

5. Saving the Mariner – Coastguard and Lifeboat Services

The 1977 lifeboat station, pictured 40 years later. It was extended in 1989 to improve crew facilities; and again in 1994 when a new crew room was added

The *Alice Upjohn* continued in service until succeeded by the *RNLB Pride and Spirit*, which operated between 1992 and 2014. This boat had the honour of being included in the London procession to mark the Queen's golden jubilee in 2002. In May 2014, Dungeness became the first station to host the new Shannon-class lifeboat, when the *Morrell* was formally installed and named at a ceremony performed by HRH The Princess Royal (Princess Anne).

Relief vessel the Jock and Annie Slater, *just after delivery to Dungeness station, in March 2014*

Crewing and launching the boats

As first reflected by the switching of the boat to Littlestone in 1861, manning a lifeboat at a remote station such as Dungeness was not always easy. At the outset there was a heavy reliance on Coastguard staff, augmented by a small number of fishermen. But an incident that occurred in 1876, just two years after the re-instatement of the Dungeness station, would have significant repercussions. Then, the Russian barque *Ilmator* got into difficulty in high seas in the west bay. Initial attempts to launch the lifeboat (the *David Hullett*) had to be shelved because most of the coastguards were on annual manoeuvres. As the barque started to break up, a large group of (mainly) fishermen and their families turned out on the beach to see what assistance they could offer. As a result of these numbers, a renewed – and this time successful – attempt was made to launch the *David Hullett*, with fishermen outnumbering coastguards on the boat. As a result, 15 sailors were plucked from almost certain death.

This incident proved to be quite a turning point. The fishing community came to realise that they were probably best placed to seize the initiative, and held the key to saving lives at sea. Although the Coastguard Service would continue to provide lifeboatmen, there was a growing acceptance that they could no longer ensure the numbers required, particularly when rationalisation of the service was undertaken in the 20th century. The fishermen embraced the extra responsibility and it became a badge of honour to serve on the lifeboat – to the extent that it soon became something of a closed shop. At one time, the crew roster was comprised solely of members of the Oiller, Tart and Richardson families. And the Bates, Brignalls, Haineses and Thomases have also been well represented over the years. There are documented accounts from some of the railway families who arrived in the 1920s (see Chapter 7), which suggest that they themselves applied for posts on the lifeboat, but were turned down

A family affair: the crew of the Mabel E. Holland, *in 1957. Within the picture are four members of the Tart family, three Oillers, and representatives of the Thomas, Richardson and Haines families*

5. Saving the Mariner – Coastguard and Lifeboat Services

without good reason. This is probably true: there were certainly some very capable and qualified "incomers" who would have been an asset to the service, but the fishermen should not be judged too harshly for this. Theirs was a tight-knit community, which took great pride in its way of life, and insularity was sometimes the flip side of the same coin.

The roll of those lifeboatmen who have received formal RNLI commendations reads like a *Who's Who* of the founding Dungeness fishing families. Douglas Oiller served as coxswain for 31 years and George (Punch) Tart for 18 years; and both were awarded the Institution's bronze medal. Tom Richard (Ben) Tart served in various capacities for 38 years (the last 18 as coxswain) and became the first at Dungeness to receive the RNLI silver medal; and Albert (Honker) Haines also served for 38 years, with four of these being as coxswain. Worthy of note here, too, is Gordon Thomas (GT) Paine, councillor and local landowner. He served as RNLI branch chairman for more than 50 years (from 1931 to 1982).

Some very influential Dungeness RNLI figures: (left to right) Doug Oiller; Tom (Ben) Tart; and lifeboat donor Ursula Upjohn (shown with GT Paine)

The Lady Launchers

No account of the Dungeness lifeboat service would be complete without paying tribute to its legendary Lady Launchers.

When an emergency arose, many of the available and able-bodied men were required to crew the boat, leaving few to launch and recover it. Accordingly, the job often and increasingly fell to the wives and daughters of the fishermen. These women were used to helping with the fishing boats, but this was a more arduous task: the wooden skids that had to be laid between the slipway and the water were of solid oak and very heavy and, on recovery, the vessel had to be hauled back up the shingle by rope, with a capstan being the only aid. For years, the equipment for the lifeboatmen themselves was very primitive compared to today's, so it was imperative that they were at least dry when they entered the boat – to mitigate the risk of hypothermia. This precluded them wading to the vessel once it was afloat, and the solution was for their womenfolk to carry them through the waters, on piggy-back! Not only

Dungeness lady launchers in action

did this require great strength, but the women would become soaked through as a result: no protective or waterproof equipment was issued to the launchers, and most had to make do with just their own overcoats and scarves.[12] To launch in wild weather, particularly in the depths of winter, and then return a few hours later in soaking clothes to help land the boat, was not for the faint-hearted.

One of the most celebrated incidents involving the Lady Launchers took place on 8 October 1932. Then, the No. 2 lifeboat, the *David Barclay*, was called out to the *Shamrock*, a London barge that had moored up in a heavy gale, but was dragging her anchor. After a distress signal had been sent, 49 people attended to help launch the lifeboat. 14 of these were regular lady launchers, but a further 12 were the wives and daughters of male launchers. Conditions were particularly brutal and, when a first attempt was made to launch, a huge gust of wind took the boat off its skids and on to the shingle. But, against huge odds, the lifeboat was launched, and an effective rescue ensued. In recognition of their efforts, the RNLI presented the Lady Launchers with an award, which was accepted on their behalf by Mrs Oiller and Mrs Brignall. A few years later, in 1953, Madge Tart and Ellen Tart (her sister-in-law) were both awarded the Institution's Gold Badge.

Most of the stories – and surviving photographs – of the Lady Launchers relate to a period between the 1930s and the 1950s, but there is documented evidence that they were first involved as early as the 1870s, albeit on a smaller scale. By 1912, there are group photographs showing up to ten women amongst the regular launchers. The tradition continued for over one hundred years, ending only in 1979, when the introduction of tractor-hauled carriages rendered teams of launchers, of either gender, obsolete. Then – at the end of the era – Doris Tart (Madge's daughter) and Joan Bates were also rewarded by the RNLI, 44 and 37 years' respective service being recognised.

---

12. The nearest thing to a uniform was a "belt" (arm band). There was a limited supply of these, and once they had been distributed amongst the Lady Launchers, any remaining ladies had to return home, or just stand by and watch.

6

Serving the Mariner – Aids to Navigation and Shipping

The currents surrounding it inevitably mean that, since man first took to its waters, Dungeness has posed dangers to mariners and their vessels. For most, thankfully, the services of coastguards and the RNLI remain a last resort. But the ever-present dangers have resulted in other services being provided, and have also presented opportunities: hovellers, for example, were effectively freelance pilots who, spotting vessels on the horizon, would row out and offer their skills to facilitate safe navigation. And some seemingly public-spirited souls (often from the fishing community), or those with deep religious convictions, would light bonfires to warn seafarers of dangers. In reality, however, there were others who had more sinister intentions, with wreckers hiding within each group. These individuals had the sole intention of luring unsuspecting mariners to their doom, purely for material gain.

The service offered by hovellers evolved into pilotage, whilst the practice of lighting fires eventually morphed into the lighthouse service. At Dungeness, there has now been a lighthouse in place for over 400 years, but, with the advent of GPS technology, these symbols of our maritime history will sadly disappear over time (Trinity House, the national lighthouse authority, is not committed to their maintenance indefinitely).

Pilotage

Expert knowledge is required to ensure safe passage through the risky Dover straits, or from the English Channel into the River Thames (and, to a lesser extent, the Medway); and highly experienced seamen with local knowledge have, for a long time, offered their services as pilots to passing ships. As early as 1526, a body – the Fellowship of the Cinque Port Pilots – was established to protect pilots and fend off foreign competition.

Members of the Fellowship would take turns piloting ships, and were required to be constantly at sea, so as not to miss any opportunity. This requirement could be hazardous and, by the end of the 1600s, there was a move to construct onshore watchtowers, from which a constant lookout could be maintained. In the following century, it became more customary for pilots to be rowed out from the shore (in the Channel this was usually from Deal or Dover). By the early 19th century, the requirement for ships to take a qualified pilot aboard had

Nanny Goat Island

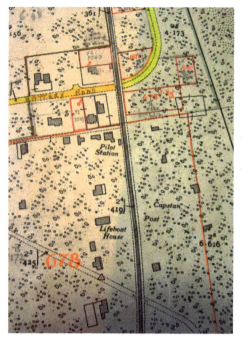

The location of the Dungeness Pilot Station, marked on a 1940 map. Note also the position of the Lifeboat House, just to the south but no longer in use (both are to the landward side of the RH&DR; see also Chapter 5). By this time, the Pilot Station was used mostly as a store and rarely accommodated pilots, although they could be rowed out to the cutter in exceptional circumstances (Map extract reproduced with kind permission of Ordnance Survey)

become formalised in law and, from 1812, two large pilot cutters were anchored off Dungeness, awaiting ships coming up the Channel. For a significant time, the task of taking pilots out to the cutter to board London-bound ships, or bringing them ashore (from where they would catch a train back to Gravesend), was contracted to local fishermen.

By the 1860s, the cutter in use at Dungeness was the *Princess*, which had a crew of five. Fourteen pilots[1] would be taken out to the cutter, and "the next one off the rank" would board passing ships as required. This was very much a lottery: pilots at the back of the roster might spend many days on board the cutter awaiting a job; or all might be employed the same day, necessitating more pilots being summoned from Dover. At this stage, the Cinque Port Pilots and Trinity House were separate entities and, in a spirit of compromise, it was agreed that ships bound for London should receive Cinque Ports pilots, with ships going in the opposite direction using Trinity House employees. Even these arrangements were subject to controversy, however, as the Cinque Ports pilots charged more than their Trinity House counterparts – and many ship owners anyway resented the principle. Once a pilot had boarded a ship, he would hoist an identifiable flag, so that a vessel without a pilot could be easily recognised. If a ship managed to avoid the cutter, there would be pilots on duty at Thanet, Dover and Deal shore stations, who would intercept it. In such cases, a pilot on duty at one of the shore stations would be rowed out to the pilot-less ship, and heavy fines were imposed on any vessel trying to avoiding pilotage in this way. The 1872 Merchant Shipping

---

1. All pilots were required to have achieved the rank of captain or above (which remains the case today).

6. Serving the Mariner – Aids to Navigation and Shipping

Act altered the way charges were levied by Cinque Ports Pilots, and the new Act also established "choice pilotage". By this, ship owners were empowered to engage *any* registered pilot, and it resulted in the (cheaper) Trinity House pilots now being routinely used to bring their ships up the Channel to London, as well as for the return journey.

Bad weather inevitably made life uncomfortable for the Dungeness pilot crews, although there was at least the opportunity to take shelter in the lee of the land – an option not available at some other stations. Unfortunately, its fixed position in a major shipping lane made the cutter vulnerable and, on 22 May 1862, the *Princess* was run down with the loss of two lives. In 1873, following the introduction of steam propulsion, a new cutter was anchored off Dungeness. In 1891, two purpose-built pilot cutters – the *Pioneer* and the *Guide* – were delivered. These were officially based at Dover for coaling and provisions, but alternated at the Dungeness station (being formally known as London No. 1 and London No. 2 Cutter respectively). Larger than their predecessors, they were each manned by five officers and eight crew, and took up to 24 pilots at any one time. Two sailing ketches (No. 3 *Wellington* and No. 4 *Vigilant*) were utilised as tenders to the Dungeness cutters and a building established on the shore to facilitate administration and house provisions. Various redeployments were made over time to reflect organisational changes and, with the introduction of a third new cutter in 1914, *Guide* was sold to Canada, with *Pioneer* being relegated solely to tender duty at Dungeness. In 1924, the *Pioneer* was renamed the *Preceder*,[2] which resulted in a new Dungeness vessel being named *Pioneer*. By this time, foreign competition was beginning to have a huge impact on pilotage, with a German pilot cutter regularly moored in the channel and working at rates that significantly undercut those of Trinity House – prompting the latter to petition the government. The need to row pilots out to the cutter at short notice continued, but by this time George Bates had cornered this particular local market.

---

2. The original *Pioneer* would continue in pilot service for another 11 years, before being broken up in 1935.

The caption to this late 1920s/early 1930s postcard reflects the signal system established at Spion Kop to communicate with the pilot cutters

The outbreak of WWII brought fresh dangers and hardships to the pilot service, although, very soon after, the Dungeness station was closed and the service moved to the contraband control zone in the Downs. It reopened after the war, when the service sold off the old steamers and re-organised duties, with tenders now having two crews, which alternated, 24 hours on and 24 hours off. Cutters would spend two weeks at Dungeness, followed by a week at Dover, then a week at the Sunk (off Felixstowe), before returning to Dungeness. By the mid-1950s, the *Bembridge* had become the dedicated Dungeness tender, soon to be replaced by the *Pathfinder* – which proved to be the last of the Dungeness-based vessels. By this time, London docks – whilst still busy – were diminishing in importance and there was a growing realisation of the need to rationalise services. The writing was on the wall and when, subsequently, the decision was taken to terminate the practice of boarding pilots from a cruising cutter, the Dungeness station closed permanently in April 1967. There are reports of some of the older pilots shedding tears as the *Pathfinder* sailed away from Dungeness for the last time.

Duties were then taken over by 40-foot launches operated directly from shore, from Folkestone and Ramsgate ports. Now, pilot services on this part of the coast are operated from Dover, with London pilots still based at Gravesend.

Trinity House and the Dungeness Lights

A first lighthouse: 1615–1635

Advances in marine technology during the 16th and 17th centuries led to a large increase in both the number and the size of ships using the English Channel. By this time, Dungeness was already a huge shingle foreland, extensive enough to cause numerous shipwrecks, with much loss of both life and cargo.

6. Serving the Mariner – Aids to Navigation and Shipping

It was Rye jeweller John Allen who first suggested a formal light at Dungeness, although Trinity House[3] rejected his proposal and declined an invitation from the King's Privy Council to erect one. Allen's idea was then taken up by William Lamplough, Clerk of the Royal kitchen, who had a most useful contact in the form of Sir Edward Howard – who held a senior Admiralty post and had the ear of King James I. Faced with these big guns, Trinity House withdrew its opposition and, after receiving approval (to private ownership) from the King, a light was erected in August 1615. This was significantly to the west of its successors, standing near the site of the current Dengemarsh sewer outfall at Pen Bars. It was a basic wooden tower, probably no more than 35 feet high, with a storage area at the base and a wooden ladder on the inside leading from the ground to a coal brazier at the top. Fuel had to be pulled up from outside in a bucket by means of a simple pulley; arrangements were hardly robust and, as a result of a combination of weathering and fires, the tower had to be reconstructed numerous times.

Lest it be considered that Howard's motive in taking forward Lamplough's idea was totally philanthropic, the royal licence entitled him to levy tolls of one penny per ton from all passing ships over the next 40 years. This was – potentially – hugely lucrative, but in practice the dues proved difficult to collect. Because of this, Howard made over all his rights to Lamplough, who used his contacts to enlist the help of Customs officials to collect the money at ports. This incensed shipowners, who could no longer avoid paying the tolls, and in 1621 they joined forces with Trinity House to promote a bill suppressing the lighthouse. This was ostensibly on the grounds that its poor light quality, rather than aiding shipping, was more "a nuisance to navigation". There would certainly appear to have been some legitimacy to this claim as, because of the difficulty of transporting coal to the 'Ness, candles had by now been substituted for fire. Parliament was reluctant to interfere with the King's licence, however, and instead warned Lamplough that the light must be improved.

In the short term, Lamplough did make enhancements, but opposition continued. This came partly from the Corporation of Rye, which, on the back of the original idea having emanated from a resident of the town, attempted to acquire the light for itself. This demonstrates that the facility was still viewed very much as a revenue earner, and the plan was to put the profits towards maintenance of the Corporation's own harbour. But efforts to secure an

---

3. Trinity House had been founded by Henry VIII in 1514 to oversee the provision of lighthouse services in England, Wales, the Channel Islands and Gibraltar.

Nanny Goat Island

Act vesting the venture in the Mayor and jurats of Rye failed and Lamplough's patent remained in force.

Second lighthouse (Lamplough's Tower) 1635–1792

Lamplough eventually had to respond to complaints about the viability and effectiveness of the tower and light and, to make matters worse, the action of the sea had resulted in it becoming significantly further from the sea, despite the passage of only 20 years. So, a more solid and conventional lighthouse was now constructed, nearer to the shore. This was on the site of what would later become the redoubt and RNSSS cottages. At 110 feet, this tower was three times the height of its predecessor. It had living quarters at the base for two keepers, and was lit by coal, requiring over a ton of the fuel to be carried manually up the tower each day.

Ownership later passed to Elizabeth Shipman, and then again to Richard Tufton – the future Earl of Thanet.[4] On his death, title passed to his daughter Margaret, the wife of Thomas Coke[5] of Holkham. Whilst a clear improvement on the original tower, the second lighthouse was still far from problem-free: mariners complained that it lacked a distinctive appearance; that the beacon was unreliable in high winds (a common and understandable affliction of all coal burners in windy locations); and that, whilst the light on the leeward side was intensely bright, visibility on the windward side was highly variable in gale conditions. It is unclear what action was taken to address these individual issues at the time, but the quality of the light came under review again in 1668, when the Elder Brethren of Trinity House summoned the licensee to appear before them and insisted that he must provide better illumination.

Third light – Samuel Wyatt's Tower 1792–1904

As longshore drift continued to change the shape of the coastline, Trinity House demanded a new light closer to the sea, and to their more exacting specifications. After some prevarica-

---

4. History of land ownership at Dungeness is explored in more depth in Chapter 11.
5. Seemingly pronounced "Cook".

6. Serving the Mariner – Aids to Navigation and Shipping

Samuel Wyatt's Tower

tion, the Coke family finally agreed. The fact that this cost in excess of £3,150 probably explains their reluctance but, to put it in context, the sum represented less than a year's worth of light dues. To the south east of the second light, it was located very close to the subsequent light (the black tower that still stands and is open to the public). At 116 feet, it was slightly taller than its predecessor and its design was based on Smeaton's classic Eddystone lighthouse. The floors and the majority of the steps were wooden, which continued to pose a fire risk, although the 18 lamps were initially powered by sperm-oil rather than coal. Sperm-oil gave way in turn to vegetable oil (obtained from turnip seed) and, later, petroleum.

Official records show some interesting details about this third light. A report from September 1817, for example, identified that a senior naval officer (Commander Popplewell), returning from Jamaica, was astonished to see that the tower was in darkness as he sailed down the Channel. This sparked a Trinity House investigation, which found that the keeper – who was 78 years old – had been unwell, and that his assistant was unreliable. The keeper was pensioned off and his assistant dismissed; but the enquiry also identified that 900 gallons of oil (as well as coal for the stove) had to be carried upstairs annually – hardly a task suited to a man of advanced years. Another report showed that the tower generated fees (light dues) of £7440 in 1819, demonstrating just what a cash cow it had become.

Although Smeaton's tower was chosen as the model because of its invincibility, this lighthouse was not built to the same exacting standards. Unfortunately, the mortar used in its construction had been mixed with saltwater and, as a consequence, by 1818 (just 26 years after its opening), the foundations were starting to crumble. Furthermore, a violent storm in Decem-

Nanny Goat Island

Quarters for keepers were constructed around the base of Wyatt's tower. These were retained when the tower was demolished to make way for the 1904 light, and remain to this day

ber 1821 caused fresh damage. A report from a commander of His Majesty's ships advised that: "lightning passed through the room where the [lighthouse keeper's] family were sitting, without injuring any person. The building has a rent from the top to bottom, visible from number 2 battery, a distance of 2 miles . . . the lantern and reflectors are damaged."

To remedy these twin problems, extra-strengthened buttresses were installed around the base of the tower, and three copper bands added to the structure. The roof – which had been leaking (resulting in the light being extinguished on a number of occasions) – was also repaired. At this time, and at the request of Trinity House, the tower was painted dark red and white.

A highly significant date in lighthouse history is 1836, for this marked the passing of an Act of Parliament that empowered Trinity House to buy out all lighthouse leases. In the case of Dungeness, Thomas Coke accepted an offer of £20,000, although in reality he had little choice (in view of the annual revenue from light dues, this was probably not a very attractive deal). In 1862, Dungeness became one of the first lighthouses to be illuminated by electric light. Around the same time, another new device was introduced – the fog trumpet. Previously, the main tools for warning mariners during times of poor visibility had been a bell (a huge item mounted on a wooden stand) and a fog whistle. The fog trumpet was something of a monstrosity, operated by compressed air and powered by steam engine. The use of tines (iron tongues of varying thickness) allowed the note of the horn to be changed to impart different messages.

Trinity House's first experiment with electricity, unfortunately, proved unsuccessful and short-lived. In its infancy, it proved problematic and highly expensive. As a result, in 1875, this form of power was replaced at Dungeness, and a massive oil lamp of 850 candle power – surrounded by glass prisms – installed. This had the effect of extending the visibility of the light to 16–17 miles. At the same time, the tower was painted black and white, to improve identification during the day.

First low light – 1884

By the late 1880s, the relentless build-up of shingle had put even the third light a significant distance from shore. Some shipping owners complained that their crews were being confused, and a number of vessels ran ashore in the east bay. A decision was thus taken to place a smaller low light near the water's edge. This was of corrugated metal mounted on timber, and had a revolving white light with a bright flash every 5 seconds – which could be seen for 10 miles. A siren-type foghorn (which had been presented to Trinity House by the United States Lighthouse Board for trials) was also housed in the same building.

Fourth Lighthouse 1904 – 1961

As the sea continued to recede, Trinity House commissioned a new light, with Messrs Pattrick & Co. of London commencing its building in 1901. Although at 319 yards from high water it was no closer to the sea than its predecessor, at 150 feet from the ground to the top of the weather vane, it was very much taller. Its construction required no less than three million bricks, and its keepers would have to climb 169 steps to reach the light.

The sheer size of this new tower meant that the building was not completed until 1904, and it was first used on 31 March of that year. Like its predecessor, in its later years it was painted in black and white bands to aid daytime identification. Although now no longer owned by Trinity House, the tower remains in situ today and forms one of the iconic images of Dungeness.[6] Initially, paraffin was used to power the light, and this was stored in tanks sunk into the shingle. This was a short-sighted move, however, as there was no gauge to identify fuel levels and estimates of supply requirements were frequently incorrect. As a result, a new tank had to be built, which was this time mounted on a plinth.

During WWI, the tower survived zeppelin bombing; and then escaped with superficial damage to the brickwork, when subjected to fighter fire in WWII. At this time, it was largely unlit – operating only when Allied convoys were passing Dungeness Point. It also accommodated a ground floor lending library for troops; it is reported that a large number of books are still outstanding!

One of the characteristics of Dungeness is that its location makes it a very important habitat for migrating birds. One of the problems encountered with the fourth light was that the beam was so bright that numerous birds were being drawn to it, crashing into the tower –

---

6. In 2015, the tower was 540 yards from high water – demonstrating that the spit had grown over 220 yards in a little over a century.

The 1904 light, with lantern prisms still in place, and well maintained

with unfortunate and inevitable consequences. In a bid to address this problem, Trinity House worked with the RSPB to install floodlighting in 1952. So successful was this measure that it was subsequently rolled out to other lighthouses. Seven years later, a second attempt was made to utilise electricity for powering the Dungeness lamp. This experiment was much more successful than the aborted trial of 1862, and this form of power lasted for the duration.

The demise of the fourth light inevitably owed something to the effects of longshore drift, but this time there was an additional factor in play. During the late 1950s, the planning process for the Dungeness A power station identified that, because of the height of the proposed new building, the navigational light would be partially obscured from the sea. Thus, a fifth lighthouse was required, closer to the sea and further from the power station. Accordingly, the

When Trinity House built the current lighthouse, the old (fourth) tower was sold to GT Paine (then owner of the Dungeness estate). It has since been sold on again and is open to the public at various times during the year. The Trinity House logo remains in place above the door

fourth lighthouse was decommissioned, becoming the tourist attraction and museum it is today (and referred to by all as the Old Lighthouse). That it is now painted entirely black is to avoid confusion with the new tower. Photographs do show, however, that there was a time, after the fifth lighthouse was operational, when both towers sported black and white hoops. It has been cynically suggested that Trinity House were not prepared to incur the expense of repainting the tower, so waited until it had been sold before insisting that the new owner made it distinguishable from its successor!

Second low light

Prior to this, by 1932, the condition of the original low lighthouse had severely deteriorated. It was deemed that it had passed the point of economic repair, so the decision made to replace it. Instead of being galvanised, the new structure had a white, brick-built cylindrical tower with an incandescent mantle. This new low lighthouse (together with a new foghorn) remained operational until 1959, when it was demolished to make way for the construction of the present lighthouse.

Fifth lighthouse (1961–date)

The location chosen for the new lighthouse – the one still in use today – was some 450 yards to the east of the 1904 light. It incorporated an electric fog signal, and initially had a range of 27 miles.[7]

At 130 feet in height, it is shorter than its predecessor, but has retained the distinctive black and white markings. These were impregnated in the concrete of the precast rings

The low light and foghorn, after replacement of the third lighthouse. Note also the old fort just visible to the left

---

7. Following re-engineering in 2000, the sealed beam light was replaced with an optic transferred from Lundy South Lighthouse, and this has had the effect of reducing the light range to 21 nautical miles.

The opening of the fifth lighthouse by the Duke of Gloucester (then Master of Trinity House) in 1961 was quite a civic occasion (left). So much so, that the authorities decided to smarten up the area. This initiative included demolishing a nearby building, Palmers Cottage (another former PLUTO building), which had fallen into disrepair since being commandeered by the army in WWII (right; Doug Oiller is the cyclist). Both photos: Chris Shore collection

(manufactured in nearby Rye Harbour) rather than being painted on subsequently, a move that has saved a considerable sum on repainting. The distinctive tall and slim design, considered to be ground-breaking at the time, was by Ronald Ward & Partners, and the new light came into operation on 20 November 1961. The following year, the tower became floodlit, not only to reduce the bird mortality rate, but also to assist identification from the seaward sides. Converted to automatic operation in 1991, it has from this point been controlled and monitored from Trinity House's central Planning Centre in Harwich, Essex. In March 2003, Grade II listed status was bestowed upon it.

Trinity House Research/Experimental station

Trinity House's interest in Dungeness has not been restricted to its pilotage and lighthouse operations, and for many years it maintained a national Experimental Station here.[8] Although the organisation insists that its first field trial facility was not established until 1958, some individuals have recollections of this being in place many years before. Older maps show buildings on the site, and identify an experimental station between the wars; and there is also evidence of the army using the facility throughout WWII. A foghorn house is shown here on maps of 1871, too, and other indicators discussed above further point to experimental work significantly predating the 1950s. Part of the explanation may be that the Admiralty also conducted experiments here; they certainly owned a significant tract of land in the vicinity. However, Trinity House surely had a greater interest, and also a land holding. It seems more likely that Trinity House were undertaking experimental work prior to 1958 (possibly in conjunction with the Admiralty), but that this was not so formalised.

Irrespective of timings, the Trinity House facility was used to test a range of marine and

---

8. Sometimes referred to as just "The Research Station".

6. Serving the Mariner – Aids to Navigation and Shipping

The fifth tower, pictured in 2015 (left) and the prototype of a Trinity House foghorn, still in place in 2018 (right)

signal apparatus for national roll-out, including technology for the first unmanned lighthouse, fog horns, light beam ranges and the use of water-cooled transistors. It was one of three such stations funded and operated by Trinity House, the others being in London (Blackwall) and the Isle of Wight (Cowes).

Other innovative work undertaken by Trinity House down the years has included the opening of a wireless fog signal in July 1929 – with Dungeness sharing (with Orford Ness) the honour of being the first location to use this equipment. The previous year, a directional wireless station, which relied on new loop system (as opposed to beacon) technology to communicate between shipping and other stations, had been introduced; this slashed costs for vessel owners. Dungeness was not the pioneer here, however, as it followed in the footsteps of stations at North Lundy, Scilly Islands, the Casquets and Start Point.

The Dungeness research facility operated until the end of the 1980s, although used only sparingly in its latter years. After this, it was utilised as a store, which soon became badly neglected. Although now a converted private residence, comprising a series of eco-friendly buildings (which have attracted a lot of media attention – see Chapter 11), a number of the historic elements – including a radio tower, fog horn prototype and small section of rail track – have been preserved and can still be readily identified. Also still distinguishable is the small, squat building which formerly housed the compressors used to charge and test foghorns (staff being sent out to sea to listen to the different types of horn, to test their effectiveness).

The former Trinity House Experimental Station, with rail track still clearly in place (2016)

Alongside the research facility, there was also a meteorological compound, in existence from the end of the 19th century. This provided key Met. Office data for many years. Part of it remains in place at the time of writing, including the base of a communications aerial

Other Navigational Aids & Services to Shipping

Not all seafarers have always been reliant on pilotage and the lighthouse service to negotiate safe passage. Those who earn their living from beach-based fishing boats have also needed to be sure that they can plot their safest course back to the beach, negotiating the dangerous currents and channels. Prior to the advent of GPS technology, this was achieved through the use of more primitive techniques. Also in times gone by – when aids to navigation and technology were relatively crude – there was a greater need for salvage services. This was particularly the case with vessels whose captains came too close to the point and became stranded.

6. Serving the Mariner – Aids to Navigation and Shipping

Other services may not have been so critical in terms of safety or survival, but have still fulfilled a need, whether in terms of communicating trade requirements, passing messages to passengers or simply replenishing provisions.

Lloyds Signal Station

Whilst the Admiralty had had their network of Signal Shore Stations to assist in the deployment of the navy fleet, there was no equivalent service that allowed the owners of merchant fleets to communicate with their vessels. Apart from issues of safety, as international trade developed there was an increasing need for owners to stay in touch with their ships' masters, and for ports to be forewarned of the arrival of goods. There was often fierce competition to reach ports – and hence markets – before rivals, and thus achieve higher prices. In response to this need, from the 1880s Lloyds (the marine and commercial insurers) established and operated a network of their own signal stations across the world. These connected to telegraph land-lines and relayed orders from owners, as well as allowing the taking of crew reports. Messages for passengers could also be sent, using a flag semaphore, or light signals at night. These signal stations survived until the development of ship-to-radio communication, and one was established at Dungeness.

The introduction of the Lloyds Signal Station facility coincided with the golden age of the clipper ship, and none was more famous than the *Cutty Sark*. Her great rival was the *Thermopylae* and the two were involved in a number of epic races to reach port first. Whilst the *Thermopylae* was faster over some routes, a celebrated battle between the pair took place in 1888; when returning from Australia to London with cargoes of wool, the *Cutty Sark* left port in Newcastle in New South Wales and reached Dungeness in an astonishing 71 days. Once Dungeness had been reached, the news was transmitted by Lloyds to the London markets, and the vessel owners were able to benefit to the tune of several thousand pounds – a not-so-small fortune.

The first Dungeness Lloyds Signal Station was established in 1876, but moved sites more than once – although there is again a lack of transparency within surviving records. *Lloyd's Notices* (which appeared in *Lloyd's List*) contained the following entry, on 8 October 1883:

> [The] Signal Station at Dungeness (has) been removed about half mile to the Westward of its former position, and is now located on some rising ground immediately to the rear of the Dungeness Lighthouse. The Station has now been connected by telegraph wire with the Government system, and the passing of vessels can be telegraphed to the owners direct from the point.

What is unusual about this move is that relocating from east to west bucked the trend; it was contrary to the direction of longshore drift, and the re-siting of the lighthouses has always been west to east. The details given are confusing: half a mile to the east would have put the previous site in the sea(!) but it may have been a reference to one of the Bates's cottages. George Bates was for a long time an agent of Lloyds, and the family connection may have

Lloyds Cottage, now standing right next to the power station security fence. After use as a Lloyds signal station, it was occupied by one of the main Dungeness fishing families (the Thomases) until the 1980s

started then. The new station was purpose-built, and is the building that can still be seen today, in the shadow of the 1904 lighthouse (now owned by EDF but, helpfully, still formally named Lloyds Cottage).

By 1891, the Lloyds Signal Station network was being eyed up by the Admiralty. As detailed in Chapter 5, the Admiralty's own Signal Station (lookout) system had undergone significant changes, not least in terms of purpose, since the ending of the Napoleonic Wars and there was a growing realisation that the Lloyds facilities could be of value to the Admiralty in future times of war. Accordingly, the Admiralty now undertook negotiations with Lloyds aimed at allowing Admiralty staff to work the stations in peacetime, in order that signallers could be trained for the eventuality of war. Not all stations were included within this agreement (which was only finalised in 1900), but Dungeness certainly was.[9]

Kelly's Directory of 1891 records Lloyds Signal station as being adjacent to the lighthouse, strongly suggesting that it was still operating from Lloyds Cottage at this time. From then on, timings are typically lacking in clarity – no doubt further confused by the issue of the joint working arrangements. Ordnance Survey maps of 1906 to 1940 onwards show the narrative "Coastguard Cottages (Lloyds Signal Station)" on the redoubt site. Photographs and surviving infrastructure confirm that it was here for at least a significant part of this time. Dungeness railway track plans for 1911 show a Lloyds Signal Station located close to, but to the south east of, the lighthouse (in the vicinity of the Admiralty Signal Station), whilst *Kelly's Directory* continued to record it as being adjacent to the lighthouse right up to 1913. This 1913 entry identified John Lowe as being the officer in charge of both Lloyds Signal and Dungeness Coastguard Stations. It is therefore likely that, following the later re-instatement of the

---

9. Its ongoing strategic importance was confirmed within a list of stations published in 1902; they were split into four categories, with Dungeness identified as "first class".

6. Serving the Mariner – Aids to Navigation and Shipping

This postcard (left) shows the Lloyds Signal Station operating from the old redoubt site. The chains used to secure the radio aerials can still be seen embedded in the top of the earth bank (right; 2018)

RNSSS, Lloyds followed their move southward from the redoubt, probably in part because of reduced lines of sight. This would mean that the OS narrative is at least in part incorrect (or out of date).[10]

Lloyds was a commercial organisation, so the signal stations had to be self-supporting. A financial report for 1901 showed that the Dungeness station had generated gross receipts (from shipping owners) totalling £403, easily outstripping the maintenance and running costs of £144.

Salvage

Some further confusion over the siting of the Lloyds Station at Dungeness has arisen from postcards of the 1930s, which depict "Bates Signal Station" operating from Spion Kop. Although George Bates was acting as an agent for Lloyds, at that time this was for salvage rather than for signalling purposes; the signalling services that he provided were mostly in regard to pilotage (as earlier described).

It was in the early part of the 20th century that Bates cornered the market for salvage. More widely known as "Jerry",[11] he was something of an entrepreneur and, as previously alluded to, has never really received recognition for his part in shaping the history of Dun-

---

10. This is not that unusual: OS maps of the time were commonly based on surveys undertaken some years previously. Similarly, *Kelly's Directory* often carried over narrative entries from one year to the next, without necessarily confirming that they remained correct.
11. This derived from his association with German tug boat companies during the early part of his working life. He also undertook work on behalf of the famous Alexander Towing Company of Liverpool.

geness. An interesting tale is told that demonstrates his single-minded approach to business. Seemingly always sleeping with one ear open, one night he sprang out of bed on hearing the sound of a band playing. Rightly assuming that this could only be the resident band of a liner that had strayed too close to shore, he made sure that he was the first on the scene. For each tug deployed, the operator was paid a fee; and Bates managed to secure two lines to the stricken vessel. He was just about to add a third tug, when the actions of the first two managed to release the liner from the shingle bank. Bates's reaction at missing out on a third fee was to utter a stream of expletives!

Salvage certainly seems to have been a lucrative business, and the proceeds of just one operation provided the funds for Bates's brother Graham to build three of the properties attributed to the pair. Spion Kop was one of the many properties built by them and the original intention was to sell it on. George, however, was so taken with it that it stayed in the family and he added the look-out tower to further facilitate the salvage business.

Other services

It seems that there was no limit to the services provided by the remarkable Bates family. They would supplement the work of the signal station by calling up passing Dutch vessels using an Aldis Lamp and morse code; then reporting details to the Dutch Consulate in London. As a result, Spion Kop was known locally for a time as The Dutch Consulate; although an 1891 directory shows "Dutch consul & shopkeeper, water house" under an entry for Graham Bates.[12]

There has been speculation as to whether such a service was provided for other nationalities, but this would appear unlikely, partly because it would seem natural to assume that the name of the Bates's cottage derived from the Boer War battle of 1900, which has great significance in Dutch history. Given that the Bates's work for the Dutch Consulate predated the building of Spion Kop (early in the 20th century), logic dictates that the latter was named in recognition of the income generated through the Dutch government (which may even have contributed to its building). It must be noted, however, that descendants of George Bates have questioned this assumption, suggesting that the building name was merely a play on words. The literal translation of Spion Kop is "spy hill" and, according to this account, the building is so-named because the elevated look-out tower (the "hill") was used to "spy" on shipping to ensure that Bates could be first to spot the need for salvage, or a pilot, and thus "cop" the business. Although there is no official record of when this service to Dutch vessel owners ceased, Ken Oiller recalls[13] that the Bates family were still involved for "many years" after the end of WWII. Subsequent inhabitants of Spion Kop have confirmed that Dutch coins have been regularly found in the garden and surrounding shingle.

---

12. This suggests that the service was another started by George Bates's father (Graham senior) from the family home.
13. Within *Dungeness Remembered*.

6. Serving the Mariner – Aids to Navigation and Shipping

Spion Kop in the 1930s (left). This post-dates the "Bates Signal Station" postcard of the same building and, whilst still at this time being used for the same purpose, it now incorporated a small post office. It remains very recognisable in 2018, although the surrounding vegetation has increased significantly

Yet another service provided by Graham Bates was the provision of crew members for ships – probably, once again, acting in his capacity as an agent for Lloyds. And, if further evidence of the Bates's entrepreneurial spirit is required, George's wife, Agnes, opened a small post office at Spion Kop – often helping out her neighbours financially when times were hard.

Fishing and beach landing aids

The fishing community has for long used its local knowledge to negotiate the dangers presented by these waters. For many years, fishermen were in the habit of charting their positions in relation to the spire of Lydd church and other prominent land features. This enabled them both to find their sea marks and to ensure the right angle of approach when returning to shore – highly important in rough weather. However, the construction of the power station greatly compromised this practice, as it partially obscured these landmarks. The solution to this new problem was the construction of two artificial and highly distinctive aids to navigation: one in the form of a letter T (on the eastern beach); and the other a diamond (on the western shore). Since inception, however, sight lines have deteriorated still further, necessitating a further structure – this one denoting a letter X. When viewed from the sea, the relative positioning of these marks confirms the optimum approach back to shore (in the case of the T, apparently, alignment with the new lighthouse is the key). Today's fishing fleet is, of course, fitted with sufficient technology and gadgetry to render such old-fashioned aids redundant, but they have been preserved as part of the unique living history of Dungeness, and are still used by recreational fishermen.[14]

---

14. They are maintained by EDF, continuing an arrangement made when the power stations were commissioned.

Nanny Goat Island

The strange aids to navigation to be found on the east and south beaches. In true Dungeness spirit, nature has improvised – with a pair of jackdaws building a nest within the "T" in 2016 (left)

Decca Research Station

The Decca Research Station – or Wireless Shed – which stood for many years on the beach next to the Experimental Station site – was not a part of either Trinity House or Admiralty operations, but arguably aided the lives of those at sea, via the medium of improving radio communication. It has been widely reported that, from here, Gugliemo Marconi – the inventor of radio – sent the first message across the English Channel in 1899. Unfortunately, this is not verified by any officially endorsed biography of him. What is certain is that the fledgling Decca Radar Company used it as a research station, although this was some years later. It is possible that it may have been used for radio experiments before this and even that Marconi – whose work took him all over the United Kingdom – did conduct some experiments at Dungeness. But this is a long way from demonstrating that the first cross-Channel radio

6. Serving the Mariner – Aids to Navigation and Shipping

The Marconi Radio Shed/Decca Building pictured (left) when still in use (Chris Shore collection) and (below) the crumbling exterior and interior in 2017

message originated from here. It would seem that the confusion has probably arisen from the Marconi company subsequently acquiring the building.

As this strange-looking building gradually fell further and further into decay, it became another of the Dungeness iconic landmarks. For reasons that will mystify many, it was in much demand as a background for fashion shoots. Man finally completed the job started by nature, with what remained of the structure being demolished in 2018. A private dwelling has now been constructed on the site.

The Watering House

There is another building at Dungeness that deserves mention in relation to the provision of services to shipping. The distinctive brick-built building that stands at the entrance to the Dungeness estate is the Watering House, constructed in the mid-19th century to accommodate the family that supplied fresh water to passing vessels. It replaced an earlier building serving the same purpose on the site.[15]

The principle of watering houses such as this was that water would be pumped up to the top level to facilitate subsequent dispense by gravity. Hence, this was (and remains) the tallest

---

15. There is reference to a Watering House here in the 1841 census, and the likelihood is that it existed for some time prior to this.

The Watering House

domestic building at the northern end of the 'Ness, with water being drawn from a natural well within the grounds of the property. At the time, the Watering House was very close to the shore and ships would moor nearby. The facility provided an attractive alternative to a well that was about 100 yards east of Pen Bars (possibly sunk by the Admiralty and which appeared on ships' charts).

For many years, the Watering House was run by the Bates family, who additionally built up a business providing fuel and other provisions (bunkerage) to ships. It was through these activities that they became (literally) the first port of call for many ships' crews and developed the contacts with owners and agents that would allow them to diversify subsequently. When Sion Kop was built (which was by then closer to the sea), many services were transferred there – as previously identified.

7

Cometh the Railway – Plans for Development; Rail and Other Transport

Channel tunnel and new ferry terminal proposals

Despite the growing fishing community, Dungeness remained pretty wild and untamed throughout the 1800s. Yet, towards the end of the century, extraordinary negotiations were taking place which had the potential to totally revolutionise the area. In the event, although the transformation did not materialise, there was still a long-term impact.

For most, mention of a railway at Dungeness conjures up images of the Romney Hythe & Dymchurch line, but this is very much the new kid on the block. For, incredible as it may seem, in the 1870s there was a battle between two major companies for the right to construct a standard-gauge railway to serve this wasteland. In other circumstances, this could have been explained by the mania for railway building that existed at the time. It would not, for example,

A postcard from the 1930s, showing both the RH&DR and branch lines in situ. Note the run-around points, buffers and Admiralty siding on the branch line

have been the first time that either of the two companies involved – the London Chatham & Dover Railway (LC&DR) and the South Eastern Railway (SER) – would have built a line for no other reason than to prevent its rival from staking a claim, regardless of its viability. In this case, however, the reason was even more unlikely.

For, at this time, Dungeness was being seriously considered as the site for a major new harbour, which would be the gateway to the continent. And this was not even the first time that it had been potentially cast in such a role. The Channel Tunnel may not have opened until 1994, but plans for an undersea crossing were first put forward in the Napoleonic era. Even from these early times, it was assumed that Dover would be the logical tunnel starting point on the English side, but, in 1865, the engineer George Remington prepared detailed plans for a railway tunnel from Dungeness to Cap Gris Nez and Boulogne. These plans were so advanced that they were lodged with the Board of Trade, and copies sent to the French Minister of Works in Paris.

Remington's proposals were partly based on the geology here presenting few difficulties in construction, and the Wealden clay that would be extracted providing a good source of material for the manufacture of good quality bricks, whereas the route from Dover would present huge problems in terms of keeping water under pressure from seeping through the porous chalk beds into the excavations. Remington himself had considerable experience in this field, having previously worked on porous rock excavation on behalf of the Admiralty in Bermuda – so was a man to be listened to.

The case was certainly well argued, prompting the *Kentish Chronicle* to write:

> We think the statement appears to contain so much matter of fact as to place the project of a tunnel under the Channel entirely in new light, and beyond doubt as to the practicability and reasonable cost, considering the great object to be obtained, and the enormous traffic which would be certain to arise, as the line would effect [an] unbroken chain of communication between England and the whole continent of Europe. Looking at the plan [of] the Channel, it must, we think, strike every one that [this] appears [to be] the proper point of departure for a tunnel to unite England and France by railway.

This article appeared on 15 September 1866 and, seven years on (in 1873), the project was still very much alive in principle, with the fledgling Rye & Dungeness Railway & Pier Company authorised to construct a railway line from Rye to Dungeness, together with a port and pier.

Appledore–Dungeness branch line

The reasons for these plans not coming to fruition are not recorded. Many other proposals for a channel tunnel were also abandoned, however, before work did finally start near Dover in 1988 – and in nearly all cases it was finance that was the stumbling block. The basic premise behind Remington's plan was to create the shortest and quickest journey between

7. Cometh the Railway – Plans for Development; Rail and Other Transport

Dungeness station pictured (left) in 1910. Although the building structure appears to be quite robust, it was up against the severe challenges posed by the harsh climate of Dungeness – the impact of which is captured by this 1962 picture of its decay (picture courtesy of Terry Tracey)

London and Paris and it was this same vision that, in the late 1870s, saw Sir Edward Watkin, Chairman of the SER, propose developing a new cross-Channel steamer service between Dungeness and the French fishing port at Le Treport. The first part of this scheme would be realised in December 1881, with the completion of the railway line between Appledore and Dungeness, which provided a connection with Hastings–Ashford services. At this time, passenger services only ran as far as Lydd, with the section onward to Dungeness restricted to freight traffic. A year and a half later, in April 1883, Dungeness station was also formally opened to passengers. Station facilities were understandably limited but, for all that, better than could be realistically have been expected by the few patrons that would require them. There was a ticket office, and both waiting and ladies' rooms. The latter included a toilet, whilst men had to make do with outside facilities comprising a separate urinal and lavatory. Engines would typically travel tender-first from Lydd – providing a very uncomfortable footplate ride in bad weather – and then run round via a simple loop at the station, to return conventionally.

In June 1882, under the auspices of the South Eastern Railway,[1] authorisation was given to extend the line from Lydd to New Romney & Littlestone,[2] and in June 1884 the New Romney extension was opened to traffic. The rationale underlying this section was not far removed from that of the Dungeness line: a grand future had been mapped out for Littlestone (which included a pier[3]), notwithstanding that its station was a mile from the coast.

Ballast Hole and Admiralty Sidings

Part of Sir Edward Watkin's vision involved utilising the virtually inexhaustible local supply of shingle. He reasoned that the shingle dug out to create the harbour and docks could be sold

---

1. Operating under the name of The Lydd Railway Company.
2. The suffix "on-Sea" was added in 1888.
3. Predictably this, too, failed to materialise.

Nanny Goat Island

Steam locomotive and train at Dungeness, c. 1930

on for track ballast and building purposes. Although the scheme would never be self-financing, he argued that this by-product could significantly mitigate construction costs. Accordingly, sidings were laid to the area identified for initial excavation, and there was a gated entrance. The ballast operation lasted only a few years (into the 1920s), but made quite an impact on the environment. The area excavated remains a shallow bowl today, some eight feet below that of the surrounding terrain in places. The most dramatic consequence of this early shingle extraction was regular autumn and winter flooding of what is still known to older residents as the Ballast Hole. In an act that would now be derided as industrial vandalism, the railway company also part-filled the Ballast Hole with spoil and waste material from its Ashford Works.[4] Large pockets of rubble and slate within the Ballast Hole area still bear testimony to this action today.

But it remains a moot point just how useful this particular resource was. The round stones were not particularly stable and made poor quality ballast, even to the extent that this was cited as a contributory factor in the 1927 Sevenoaks rail crash. This seems harsh, in that it was surely the engineers who should shoulder the blame for any inappropriate use of materials, rather than the geological source.

The only other branch line siding at Dungeness was laid down later than those serving the Ballast Hole. Most sources state that the Admiralty siding came into being around 1920, but there is little to confirm this. Maps were not updated and re-issued as frequently as is now the case, but it can be confirmed that the siding was not in existence in 1911; and photographs from the mid-1920s show it to be then well established.

---

4. Many locals followed suit, using it as an unofficial rubbish tip.

7. Cometh the Railway – Plans for Development; Rail and Other Transport

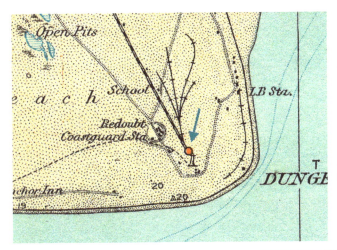

Section of 1907 OS map showing the sidings leading to the Ballast Hole. The other track (tramway) shown around the headland was laid in the 1890s to enable the lifeboat to be launched from the south beach if weather conditions demanded (but was not greatly used). The Admiralty siding was not in place at this time (Map extract reproduced with kind permission of Ordnance Survey)

The northern edge of the Ballast Hole (left) and sleeper evidence of one of the former sidings that served it (both 2018)

The Admiralty siding was effectively an extension of the branch line, separated from it by a gate. It ran from the station past the lighthouse, closely following the route of the current road, passing in front of the site that would later accommodate the relocated Britannia Inn, and ending close to the fog station (the site of the 1961 lighthouse). Although the question of its naming ought to be easy to answer, like many other issues at Dungeness it is not. The Admiralty siding served a number of different clients, including Trinity House, a crushing plant and the fishing community. The only Admiralty function at the time would have been the Signal Station, which was set back a little from the line. This is puzzling, as it would have been more usual for the name of the siding to reflect the furthest point that it served – i.e. the fog station. It is just possible that the fog station was incorrectly perceived to be operated by the Admiralty rather than Trinity House and that the name attributed was an informal one.

The crushing plant, 1904 lighthouse and Admiralty siding in 1924 (Top – Chris Shore collection) and (bottom) the same view in 2017. The building on the left is the Decca Research Station, subsequently (in 2018) demolished

It may even be that the Admiralty was working with Trinity House on some its experimental work, which would also account for the confusion over ownership of the Experimental Research station, as discussed in Chapter 6.

The existence of a crushing plant adjacent to the Admiralty siding is also the source of much debate. It has been mooted that this demonstrates that aggregate was processed alongside ballast or that, after ballast extraction ceased, gravel working took over. There is also doubt over exactly when the plant was built, and few photographs of it exist. The one reproduced here dates from 1924 (the plant being clearly visible at the bottom right-hand corner). Yet even this is surrounded by confusion: some have suggested that the state of the plant indicates that it was falling apart by this time, whilst others argue that it is shown under construction, or even that part of the roof and sides were removed to limit the levels of dust inhaled by workers.

The size of the plant is certainly not indicative of any large-scale operation. The reality may be that it served only a small and specialised stone industry. This involved the processing of rarer stones (particularly blue flint[5]) used in the manufacture of ceramics and costume

---

5. Still to be found on the beach today, blue flint stones are white on the outside and dark on the inside, with a rough texture.

7. Cometh the Railway – Plans for Development; Rail and Other Transport

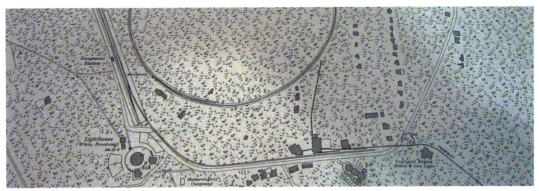

This 1946 OS map shows the network of lines leading to and from the crushing plant (which is the middle of the three linked buildings shown, lower right centre). The beach tramway is visible at the bottom right (extract reproduced with kind permission of Ordnance Survey)

Foundations of the crushing plant, weighing station and related buildings, still visible in 2018

jewellery, and which were often uncovered by sea action. These stones would be placed into skips and then pushed up the beach manually to the crushing plant, using another tramway on the beach, which connected to the Admiralty siding. Surprisingly, this activity did provide (meagre) full-time employment for a few individuals, particularly in the depression of the 1920s and 30s. Although records are largely lacking, a Mr C. Oiller was registered as a licensee for the collection of flints in 1921 – strongly suggesting that the crushing plant was established by then.

The Admiralty siding saw ever-diminishing volumes of traffic, and it has been reported that its final significant act, ironically, was to provide materials for the building of the last section of the estate road. These materials were tipped direct from the railway wagons, which accounts for the road being constructed so close to and parallel with the railway. The siding did, however, remain in place until 1952, when the rest of the Dungeness branch line was lifted (see also below).

Two views of the former Admiralty siding track bed, parallel to the estate road (2017)

The base of the Dungeness crushing plant, together with remnants of other related buildings, can still can still be seen today, although the remains of wartime fortifications and the subsequent construction of the current Britannia public house have clouded the issue. The former trackbed of the Admiralty siding can also still be clearly seen next to the estate road, slightly sunken and with tell-tale signs of clinker quite prevalent along its route.

Lydd Crushing Works

Whatever its status, the Ballast Hole did not hold anything like a monopoly over the extraction of ballast and gravel in the vicinity. A number of different sites have been worked over the years, and some of these have since been returned to nature, as detailed in Chapters 9 and 11. On the western edge of the Dungeness National Nature Reserve (but to the north of the Lydd–Dungeness road) is the ARC pit, and slightly to the north west of this are the Water Tower pits, which were formerly served by the Lydd Crushing Works. This was a much more heavily used facility than the works at Dungeness Point, but was also dependent on the railway, and had its own dedicated siding with loading equipment. The extent of this infrastructure lends credibility to the view that the crushing plant at Dungeness would not have been sufficient to host its own meaningful aggregates services.

The Reality

It soon became clear that – as with Remington's before him – Watkin's dream would never reach fruition, and the ferry port scheme was fully abandoned in the early years of the 20th cen-

7. Cometh the Railway – Plans for Development; Rail and Other Transport

The much larger and more heavily used crushing plant was between the original and re-routed New Romney junction (near to the 1902 water tower – as shown on this 1940 map (left) (reproduced with kind permission of Ordnance Survey). Evidence of the plant and unloading facilities, next to the railway line, which now only serves the power station, can still be found (right; 2018)

tury. The railway company was now left with a terminus in a remote area, and a line carrying only the lightest of passenger traffic – although for residents of Dungeness it did continue to provide greater access to markets for their fish, and a means of obtaining essential provisions.

Just as Dungeness never became an international port, so the dreams for Littlestone would remain unrealised. In 1937, in an effort to cut losses and tap into the growing holiday market, the New Romney branch line (now under the auspices of the Southern Railway) was re-routed nearer to the coast. The New Romney junction was moved closer to Dungeness, with two intermediate stations opened at Greatstone and Lydd-on-Sea. At the same time, Dungeness station was closed to passenger traffic and residents told that Lydd-on-Sea station would now serve their needs. For those faced with the prospect of a mile walk on cold winter days, this was not a very satisfactory alternative.

Although closed to passenger traffic, the line to Dungeness remained in place for another 15 years, hosting ever-decreasing volumes of freight traffic on the Admiralty siding and the occasional movement of troops. Following the final closure of the section between Romney Junction and Dungeness in 1952, most of the rail was removed. But the sleepers were left in place by the railway company. Although some of these were taken by locals for firewood, the rotting remains of many can still be seen for much of the route, more than 65 years after trains last ran. Surprisingly, this also applies to the former Ballast Hole siding sleepers.

Seen from the top of the old lighthouse in 2017, the line of the old track, stretching into the distance, is still very discernible. A part has been taken over by the power station for its approach road, but connects with the extant line, which is now used solely for the exchange of nuclear flasks

The end of the line today, showing a nuclear flask about to be removed. The buffers are just short of the Dungeness Road, at Halfway Bush. Security considerations mean that the loading/unloading area is fenced and gated at each end. The 1937 New Romney branch junction was some 150 yards north of here

Dungeness station itself fared similarly. The building was allowed to decay to a point in the 1960s when what remained of the wooden structure was dismantled for firewood. The rest has just been left to wither on the vine, with no effort or desire to remove. The foundations and obvious site of the gents' toilet, as well as parts of the platform, remain very visible and, overall, what is left is perfectly in keeping with the rest of this living industrial and natural landscape.

Sale of old rolling stock

There were, however, two more lasting legacies of the unsuccessful railway gamble. The first arose from the earlier actions of SER, which had purchased 1,000 acres of land at Dungeness

7. Cometh the Railway – Plans for Development; Rail and Other Transport

The remains of the former Dungeness branch line station and platform, 2017 (left) and 2013 (right)

(for a reported £5 an acre), although the significance of this action went unrealised for a long time. The other – and much more obvious – legacy resulted from the Southern Railway offering its staff the opportunity to buy old and redundant rolling stock. The premise was that they could have these carriages transported to Dungeness, where they would be taken off the rails and be used for accommodation on land owned by the company. It seems that the policy was for them to be used only as holiday accommodation, but no great effort was made to enforce this.

The initiative resulted in a significant influx of newcomers to Dungeness in 1920 and 1921, mainly employees and families from the railways works at Ashford, many of whom

This picture, from the early 1920s, shows one of the first of the carriages transported to Dungeness, probably for use as a holiday home – despite the children wearing school uniform! (Chris Shore collection)

would decide to make their residence here more permanent. The first of the carriages to arrive was named *Samoa* by its owner (reflecting a ceremonial connection to that country) and is one of the few to have retained its original name throughout its history. These new homes were all at the southern end of the village, reflecting the problems of moving the carriages any great distance from the railway track. So, from day one, there was a division between the established fishing families at one end of the village and the new residents, who were mostly unaware of the existing culture, at the other.

It is clear from this distance that many of the new homeowners had little or no idea what they were letting themselves in for. There are some marvellous anecdotes dating from this time, and the situation is best illustrated in the words of those who were there. The following account (reproduced with permission of Mike Golding) from Mabel Lusted (born in 1912/3), who travelled down with her mother and brother in early summer 1920,[6] beautifully captures the scene. It is a wonderful piece of social history, including descriptions of the railway service, the moving of the carriages and the ballast and shingle crushing operation; it also depicts the problems caused by free-ranging goats, as well as the absence of any health and safety considerations:

> Dad and I walked miles at weekends trying to find somewhere to live. We couldn't find rooms – four children were a lot to house. In desperation Dad bought a disused railway coach and rented a piece of land at Dungeness on which to put it.[7] He was going to transform it into a bungalow.
>
> Moving day arrived; the furniture was to go by train. Freda and Thelma[8] were to stay with Aunts until Mum was settled in and Dad was staying in Ashford and joining us at the weekend. Cyril and I went off with Mum on a beautiful June morning, loaded up with cases and the babies' pushchair piled high with things we would need until the furniture arrived. There were only two trains a day to Dungeness and I think we were the only passengers on it that day. We arrived at the tiny station to find not a soul in sight and a beach stretching for miles. Cyril and I just stared at the scene. Before us was a tall lighthouse surrounded by the keepers' cottages, an old fort that was built for the 1914 war and to the left of that a lower lighthouse that also housed a foghorn. In between were a few converted railway coaches and a few fishermen's cottages dotted about. Not having a clue as to where to go, Mum knocked at the lighthouse keeper's door, asking if he knew where Mr Lusted's bungalow was; she explained that Dad had bought a railway coach but it was going to be just like a bungalow, and had rented a plot of land. The keeper looked very puzzled and said: "the latest one here is on the railway siding over there". He took us across to it and yes it had our name on it.

---

6. This is an inference drawn from accompanying information. It is clearly early summer and could have been 1921 – although 1920 seems much more likely.
7. It may be that Mr Lusted was a railway employee, but it was seemingly not his intention to treat the carriage as holiday accommodation, underlining that scant attention was paid to official railway policy.
8. Mabel's sisters.

7. Cometh the Railway – Plans for Development; Rail and Other Transport

Of course, it was high off the ground and there was no way we could climb into it. There we stood, in our best clothes, Mum wearing a posh hat trimmed with artificial fruits, very fashionable then, that she had worn so it didn't get crushed. Mr Bennett, the lighthouse keeper, left us standing there saying he would see what he could do. After a time he returned with a large wooden sleeper that he managed to prop up against the door. Mum climbed up, fitted the key in and opened the door expecting to find the compartments upholstered so that we would at least be able to make our beds up on the seats until the furniture arrived; but what a sight met our eyes. Each compartment was stripped of fabric and padding. They were just large, bare shells covered in soot and grime from the steam trains, with tin tacks sticking out everywhere. We looked in disbelief! After our lovely, spotless home we were faced with these sooty, dirty compartments.

When Mum had recovered from the shock she said: "It's no use crying, we will have to do the best we can". We sorted out some older clothes, carefully folding the ones we had been wearing and piled them up with all our luggage beside the railway line. There was only one track. Mr Bennett was most helpful and lent us a hammer, pinchers, a bucket and several other useful things. We found a well nearby and set to work trying to get a couple of compartments reasonably clean. Sweeping soot and pulling out tacks we didn't notice the goats who had collected around our luggage and saw them just as one goat was munching Mum's best hat. All that was left were the fruits and the brim hanging from his mouth. "My hat!" shouted Mum, but Cyril and I just collapsed with laughter, it looked so funny. The goats had eaten quite a few things and we chased them off and stowed what was left in one of the compartments.

We were nearing teatime and Mum sent Cyril and I off to find driftwood along the shore. We came back with as much as we could carry and Mum made a hole in the beach and managed to make a fire and boiled up some water for tea. Then we scrubbed and cleaned until daylight began to fade. Having got two compartments reasonably clean we made up a bed of sorts on the floor. Mum in one and Cyril and I next door. We talked far into the night. We both felt scared. It was quite eerie for, as the light from the lighthouse revolved, everything lit up and the old fortress looked dark and sinister. We felt scared, too, for our future.

Tired out we eventually fell asleep when suddenly we were awakened by a loud crash and we shot across the floor. Grabbing each other, our hearts pounding, we continued to look out of the window and found Mum was doing the same. We were being shunted along the railway track. I don't know who was most astonished, the engine driver or us. He climbed down from the engine and came and spoke to Mum who explained why we were there. "Sorry Missus" he said, "I've come to load up with ballast. There is no siding here so you'll have to come with us. I'll uncouple you when I've finished". This happened several nights!

We seemed to be pulling tacks, scrubbing and cleaning for days. We then learned that our furniture had been sent to Scotland by mistake and was somewhere on the railway line.

Eventually, Dad, with some friends to help him, moved the coach to our plot of shingle. After much heaving and struggling they managed to get it off the line and onto

Not the Lusted family, but William and Florence Cole – who arrived on the scene only slightly later

long round poles and pulled and tugged it across the beach and into position, a foot or so above the shingle, resting on thick heavy railway sleepers. When this was accomplished we gave a loud cheer. Now we could start turning it into a home. Fortunately Dad had found a site near a fresh water well. Cyril and I had to make sure there was always water for us; to do this we had to stand astride the top of the well and throw the bucket down. When it reached the bottom we had to give a sharp tug and haul the water up. How we didn't fall in I shall never know as in wet weather the planks of wood on which we stood were extremely slippery.

Dad's first job was to build a loo; this was a wooden structure with an Elsan chemical closet. Next he knocked out some of the partitions in the carriages, making two large rooms and one small one. Mum and Dad had the small room and the other two were a living room and bedroom which we children shared. We scraped and painted and papered until all was ready for when our furniture arrived. There was no gas or heating of any kind and so Mum built a little fire on the beach and on this she managed to boil the water and produce a meal for us. Cyril and I got up early each morning to find driftwood along the shore to keep the fire going. Mum improvised and always managed to make us a hot meal of some sort. She was just incredible!

Eventually the furniture came. It was heaven to sleep in a bed again. The floor seemed to get harder every night. Freda and Thelma joined us now so once more we were all together.

Most of the carriages were standard third class passenger stock, dating back to around the turn of the century, although some wagons were additionally utilised. The latter were most commonly employed to form a link between two carriages – as still evidenced by Caithness –

7. Cometh the Railway – Plans for Development; Rail and Other Transport

Some carriages have a more illustrious history than their neighbours. Providence *(originally called* Windwhistle, *but with other incarnations in between) is believed to have once been Queen Victoria's private railway carriage*

To facilitate the removal of carriages from the track, poles were inserted underneath to allow them to be lifted to their allocated places on the shingle. The picture shows a wagon being moved in this way (Chris Shore collection)

although occasionally made dwellings in their own right. The property known as *Jesmond* (close to the new lighthouse), for example, was developed around a former guard's van. More specifically, its very near neighbour, *Sulaco*, started life as a five-ton fruit and milk van on the Somerset & Dorset Joint Railway.

One of the drawbacks with railway carriage accommodation of this vintage, of course, is that it is predominantly wooden, and vulnerable to fire. The property belonging to the Everest family[9] (situated between Haford and Venture) was destroyed in this way at the end of the 1950s, when an oil-fired stove was knocked over. The plot still remains empty.

---

9. Another family who had moved from Ashford after the railway company made sites and carriages available to its employees and pensioners.

The restored Westward Ho! is the property on the left of this photograph (taken from the top of the fourth lighthouse)

The fire which destroyed the Everest family home (top; Chris Shore collection); and the still vacant plot where it stood, in 2018

7. Cometh the Railway – Plans for Development; Rail and Other Transport

Particularly where extensions have been added (protecting the exterior of the fabric), some of the original carriages are very well preserved, as this picture demonstrates. Undergoing redecoration, parts of the former paintwork of this carriage are still identifiable, and even the door and windows are original (and complete with etching)

In 1987, Westward Ho! (one of the properties to the south east of the old lighthouse) was also badly damaged by fire, but in somewhat different circumstances. Comprising two former carriages, it was being used in the making of the film *Bellman & True*, and the script required it to be blown up. For filming purposes, an extension was built and the owners assured that all necessary safeguards were in place. Whilst the realism of this scene pleased the director, however, the special effects team got it badly wrong, and the explosion resulted in major fire damage to the carriages.

Both were initially deemed to be beyond economical repair, and attempts to procure replacement carriages of this vintage (principally through local railway preservation groups) were unsuccessful. Quotes for construction of new carriages to the same specification came in at £100k, so a major reconstruction was required. For these reasons – the predominantly wooden materials and the difficulty of securing replacements – it has at times been difficult for some owners to obtain insurance cover through mainstream insurers.

Despite such problems, many of the original carriages still remain at Dungeness, over 120 years since they first entered railway service. Most have been extended or even built around, but there remains plenty of evidence of their former use. The issues of development and planning are, however, quite complex and are explored in more detail within Chapter 11.

Romney, Hythe & Dymchurch Railway

A much more successful and enduring railway story has been that of the 15″-gauge Romney, Hythe & Dymchurch Railway (RH&DR). The well-told version is that this was the brainchild of two Old Etonian racing drivers, Captain Jack Howey and Count Louis Zbrowski, although the latter was sadly killed in a race prior to their dream being realised. Howey then continued the project to build the RH&DR alone, on a site that the pair had earlier selected. The acknowledged expert on RH&DR history, WJK Davies,[10] however, maintains that this was the spin put on it by Howey himself and that, whilst Zbrowski was keen on the idea of a light railway, he died before any plans as to where to build it had been drawn up.

Regardless of which account is believed, the main significance of the choice of location was that it lay between Southern Region (SR) termini (New Romney & Littlestone; and Hythe). Howey certainly saw in this an opportunity to fill a gap in the market. But, even before the line between New Romney and Hythe opened in 1927, plans were being drawn up for an extension to Dungeness. Following a Public Inquiry, the Romney, Hythe & Dymchurch Light Railway (Extension) Order was granted on 12 July 1928, notwithstanding that it had actually opened on 24 May of that year! The spin put upon this by parts of the press is interesting, with the Railway Magazine commenting:

> So excellent are the relations between the railway and local landowners and public authorities that it was possible to carry out a considerable amount of construction in advance of the Light Railway Order from the Minister of Transport.

At this time, the extension terminated just before The Pilot Inn, where a turning "y" (or triangle) was installed.[11] Work on the remaining section to Dungeness was quickly completed, however, not least because the shingle terrain allowed the track to be laid directly onto it for the most part (only a few minor cuttings and small stretches of low embankment being required). Accordingly, Dungeness RH&DR station opened to traffic on 3 August 1928.

The line from New Romney to Dungeness is five and a half miles in length, and at this time was double tracked, with the exception of a loop on which the Dungeness station was sited. This loop arrangement precluded the need to construct a turntable at the southern terminus and it worked well. Unfortunately, complications arose when the railway was handed back to Howey by the Army at the end of WWII. The line had been so badly damaged that Howey took the decision to reduce the Dungeness track to single-track operation, but this meant that the loop could no longer be utilised in the same way. The solution was fairly straightforward: trains would continue to travel clockwise around the loop, but re-enter the

---

10. See bibliography.
11. The train from New Romney would stop between the two arms of the Y; the engine would then be detached, run forward, reverse up one of the arms and then travel down the other before reversing onto what was previously the back of the train. In this way it would now be facing the direction of travel for the return journey.

7. Cometh the Railway – Plans for Development; Rail and Other Transport

RH&DR locomotive No 9 Winston Churchill *entering Dungeness (October 2018)*

RHDR locomotive No 2 Northern Chief *with a Dungeness-bound train at Britannia Points (2016)*

single track by means of a spring-loaded point. Because of its location close to the site of the public house of the name,[12] the junction has since been known as Britannia Points.

RH&DR histories record that, for a short time (from around 1937), a spur ran from the loop to a building known as the weigh-house. This is shown on the Ordnance Survey map of 1946[13] as a separate line or tramway, but without a physical connection. Whilst it is possible that it was used for a time for gravel workings, it seems most likely that its purpose was solely for the transfer of fish, with the link to the weigh-house being key. It may also be that this had previously formed part of the skipway network, as described in Chapter 2; if so, the difference in gauges would explain the lack of linkage.

---

12. At the time, the Britannia pub was sited further to the north, as described in Chapter 10.
13. This is based on a 1940 survey, so reflects the earlier date.

Nanny Goat Island

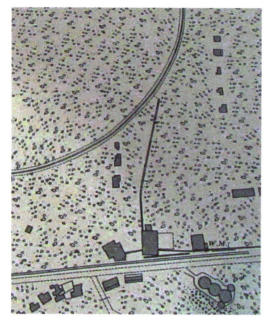

Detail from the 1946 OS map showing the spur to the crushing plant and weigh house (marked WM – weighing machine). Map extract reproduced with kind permission of Ordnance Survey

A further short siding may have run from near the Pilot Halt parallel to the shore, just above the line of high water, as also referenced in Chapter 2. An RH&DR track plan of September 1928 shows this and, whilst these plans did not always directly correspond to what was built, there is a newspaper article that refers to a "fish siding" being constructed in early 1928. If this was the case, it certainly was not in place for any great time – and the track may have been subsequently taken by the fisherman for their own network.

As with many undertakings at Dungeness, there were some high expectations which ultimately proved unrealisable. In terms of facilities, the RH&DR station was built with separate

The embankment for the RH&DR spur to the weigh-house, still quite prominent in 2017

122

arrival and departure areas, which each had their own waiting shelter. It was also fully signaled, with its own discrete signal box; but the signals were soon identified as an unnecessary luxury and were abandoned – with the box being converted to a ladies' toilet. Similarly, the waiting shelters were deemed to be superfluous and were later demolished. The booking office was more enduring, lasting until a new facility was provided in 1960. At this time, too, a new waiting shelter was constructed. This survived until 1983, when a fierce storm put paid to it: it is said that the noise created by its collapse was heard as far away as New Romney.

Road, Tracks & Paths

From the mid-19th century, Denge Marsh, Pen Bars and Galloways were linked to Lydd by relatively good quality tracks, but, from there to the Point, the only means of access was across the shingle by backstay. From the north – and even after the advent of the railways – access was similarly hampered by the lack of decent paths. There was a broad but well-used track on the shingle that was "maintained" with the use of ashes and other debris, and which ran from the site of what would become Lydd-on-Sea station to the RNSSS cottages, via the school. This predated the working of the Ballast Hole, but crossed the area in question which, even then, was prone to flooding. The path was accordingly raised, and was quite heavily used by residents. Much later, when piping to the power station was installed, it was destroyed; but, because it is one of the few legal rights of way across the shingle, was subsequently restored. The raised bed is still quite visible today, although may be mistaken for a low railway embankment.

Furthermore, the road from Lydd was only built piecemeal, first to Boulderwall Farm and then extending to The Pilot (when on its previous site at the estate entrance). It would not be until August 1935 that this coast road, linking New Romney, Littlestone and the northern fringes of Dungeness to Lydd, was finally completed. From the start of the 20th century right up until this time, the majority of provisions coming into Dungeness were delivered by rail. There have even been stories passed down of a sail-driven trolley being used to carry goods along the RH&DR line from New Romney! There were some local traders that still delivered, and those serving Dungeness at this time included the Lydd Brewer, Finn's, who utilised wide-wheeled carts[14] to move beer over the shingle. There were two of these carts specially built – essentially to service the Britannia Inn – and they would not have been cheap to make. The assumption must be that the drinking habits of the Dungeness folk more than justified the expense![15]

The completion of the coast road facilitated the building of a connecting estate road, and this work was allocated (perhaps unsurprisingly) to GH Bates of Lydd. The road was of

---

14. The wheels being 18 inches in width.
15. As with many aspects of Dungeness life, there is an alternative version of events. This is that the carts were constructed by fishermen for bringing their catch up the beach, but were subsequently bought and adapted by the brewery.

The extension of the road between Boulderwall Farm and Dungeness, in 1925. This was part of a Lydd Council scheme to provide local employment (Ted Carpenter collection)

concrete construction and was completed in 1938, although at this stage it terminated at Beach Cottage. This allowed milk to be delivered on a regular basis for the first time. Transported by lorry, the milk was collected in jugs by residents – although many complained that it was routinely watered down. Weekly deliveries of groceries and greengroceries were also now introduced (by Messrs Whites and Charlie Mannering respectively), both originating from Lydd.

The only other real developments of note regarding infrastructure have been the construction of the concrete road to service the eastern fishing beach in the late 1970s and the short cut from the south end of the estate road to the power station, past the RH&DR restaurant. The latter was funded by the Central Electricity Generating Board (CEGB), to accommodate

Barrels of beer being delivered to the Britannia pub by one of the two Finn wide-wheeled carts. Coalman George Baker would borrow one of the carts – now preserved and on display in the Lydd Museum – to make his own deliveries (photo courtesy of Ted Carpenter)

7. Cometh the Railway – Plans for Development; Rail and Other Transport

The completion of the estate road in 1938 also allowed residents access to a bus service for the first time. This was initially operated by Carey's of New Romney and ran for many years, but was never particularly frequent. This picture dates from the 1940s, and the RNSSS cottages can be seen in the background

the increasing volume of power station traffic (although, as a goodwill gesture, the public has additionally been allowed to use it). The access road from Dungeness Road down to the RSPB reserve past Boulderwall Farm was built around 1970, but remains unmetalled.

Air Transport

Lydd's Ferryfield Airport does not fall within the geographical remit of this book, although, had some of the wilder schemes for its expansion come to fruition, this position would have changed. Nevertheless, Dungeness is very much on the flight path for both Lydd airport and other channel-crossing flights. As a consequence, there have been a number of civilian aircraft casualties and peacetime incidents, in addition to the wartime losses described in Chapter 3.

On 17 June 1929, the Imperial Airways Handley Page W.10 *City of Ottawa* ditched in the sea some three miles off Dungeness after suffering an engine failure. The aircraft had been operating an international scheduled flight from Croydon to Le Bourget when a connecting rod in the starboard engine broke and the pilot unsuccessfully attempted to divert to Lympne Airport. Although seven passenger lives were lost, it was fortunate that the pilot had managed to bring his plane down within sight of the Belgian trawler *Gaby*, whose captain acted heroically in engineering the rescue of the four remaining passengers and the two crew. The survivors were taken back ashore at Folkestone by the Dover Pilot cutter and the wreckage of the plane towed to Dungeness beach, where it became something of a macabre tourist attraction.

In 1938, two accidents took place – both involving RAF craft. The first of these resulted from the increasing mania for air races (which had resulted in six forced landings on Romney Marsh over the previous six years). The pilot had to make a crashlanding at Dengemarsh but, whilst his craft was badly damaged, he escaped with only minor injuries. On 6 October of the

The recovered wreckage of the City of Ottawa *that crashed just off Dungeness beach in 1929 (photo courtesy Steve Tart)*

same year, a Handley Page HP54 RAF crew was conducting a night training exercise on behalf of the 215th Squadron. Whilst cruising over the Channel in poor weather conditions, the craft went out of control and crashed into the sea off Dungeness Point. Despite searches by both British and French authorities over several days, no trace of wreckage was ever discovered. It is believed that the aircraft may have been struck by lightning.

On 15 January 1958, a Channel Airways de Havilland DH.104 Dove was approaching the British coast on a flight from Rotterdam to Southend. Having been advised that thick fog precluded a landing at Southend, the pilot rerouted to Lydd. He was unfortunately unable to locate the runway, and a second attempt to land also had to be aborted. By now the fuel levels were dangerously low and, as both engines failed, an emergency landing was made on Dungeness beach. The craft slid for many yards before coming to rest, and was completely written off – but all seven occupants lived to tell the tale.

As has already been seen, Dungeness is not unused to outrageous and futuristic development speculation, but one outline plan put forward in November 2004 is worthy of special mention. This was for a marine-based four-runway airport in the Channel just off Dungeness.[16] Press reports stressed that this was very early days in terms of a scheme and, predictably, the proposal was quickly shelved.

---

16. Similar in nature to the more widely-publicised plans for the "Boris Island" airport proposed for the River Thames.

8

Going Nuclear – The Dungeness Power Stations

The power station ("The Candle Factory" to its neighbours) is now an integral part of the Dungeness landscape. Few would argue that it is a thing of beauty, although many have now come to accept its presence – and not always as an unpleasant necessity.

It was in 1955 that the UK government published its white paper: *A programme of nuclear power*, which announced a first nuclear programme. The following year, the world's first commercial nuclear reactor was opened at Calder Hall in Cumbria, and the government then began to search for further potential sites. The main criteria were access to abundant supplies of deep water and geographic distance from areas of dense population, so it was no great surprise when Dungeness (amongst other coastal areas of great scientific interest) was shortlisted. Test boreholes were completed in 1957 and, following a public inquiry held in December 1958, formal approval to proceed was granted in 1959.[1] Inevitably, there was much conflict between the local population on the one side and the government and developers on the other. Public relations were poorly handled and the Kent County Council Planning Team complained that they were only made aware of the scheme as late as 1957, when a press report alluded to "secret borings" in the vicinity.

---

1. This appears to have been just a nicety, as much preparatory work on the land had already been undertaken.

Construction of Dungeness A and B stations

Work on the Magnox reactor, which would become known as Dungeness A Power Station, began in August 1960. The project was undertaken by a consortium – The Nuclear Power Group (TNPG) – with Robert McAlpine designated as the main contractor.[2] Construction presented some notable engineering challenges, not least because of the shingle terrain. From an early stage, it was evident that transporting construction equipment, as well as the various pieces of plant and machinery, would cause huge problems in terms of the limited local road infrastructure. An approach road (making use of the former railway track bed) had to be constructed from the Lydd–Dungeness road at Halfway Bush, whilst other parts of the road network needed amendment. Modifications included the widening of New Romney High Street, the strengthening of the Warren road bridge over the RH&DR, and the construction of a level crossing over the railway at Lydd (to avoid overloading the bridge).

Despite all this, the remaining limitations resulted in large goods having to be floated in on huge rafts, from Dover. Because of the high water table, wells were sunk and a sheet piling "skirt" built around the site, which stretched for ¾ mile. A 400-ton Goliath crane was built on site (blown up on completion), and a platform placed 300 yards offshore to connect the seawater inlet. This was put together in Folkestone Harbour and floated to Dungeness, before being fixed to the sea bed. With great lack of imagination, it was named "The Thing".

At its peak, nearly 2,500 people were employed on the building work and a residential camp on the site housed up to 700. This was clearly not sufficient to accommodate everybody at peak times, so bed-and-breakfast establishments in the locality thrived. In the summer months, some construction workers opted to save their subsistence allowance and slept on the

Power station access road under construction, August 1960

---

2. The main sub-contractors included Balfour Beatty, CA Parsons, AEI, Whessoe, Reyrolles and John Thompson.

8. Going Nuclear – The Dungeness Power Stations

The Goliath crane in situ, during construction of Dungeness A

beach. The camp itself included shops and a cinema. After five years, work was finally complete, and electricity generation commenced in 1965. Although it was scheduled to operate for only 25 years, Dungeness A was to function for over 40, eventually closing in December 2006. Its last year was also its most productive.

One of Dungeness A's enormous boilers arriving on site, by sea (left; Chris Shore collection); and part of the infrastructure around the original admin blocks, pictured in December 2017 (right). This is periodically exposed by the action of the tide, which well reflects the impact of longshore drift

Dungeness A under construction (Chris Shore collection)

The expansion of the government nuclear programme meant that existing sites with room for growth were top of the list for further development. In the case of Dungeness, electricity generation had barely begun when the contract for a second station (Dungeness B) was placed, in August 1965. Over the intervening five years, however, there had been some significant industry changes, in terms of technology, administration, costs and expectations. The new contract was for £89m and was again awarded to a consortium, but not TNPG; instead, it went to Atomic Power Construction (APC), working under the supervision of CEGB's General Development and Construction division. Work on site commenced in January 1966, with the initial expectation that commercial operation would begin in 1970 – a highly optimistic projection.

In contrast to Dungeness A, the new plant – the UK's ninth nuclear station – was to feature advanced gas-cooled (as opposed to Magnox) reactor technology. This was the first of the commercial scale advanced gas-cooled reactor (AGR) power stations, with a design based on the much smaller prototype (the WAGR design) developed at Windscale and comprised two reactors. Unfortunately, those who felt that the experience of both the earlier Dungeness station and the Windscale experiment would expedite the completion of Dungeness B, were badly mistaken. Scaling up of the Windscale prototype presented many problems, the most significant of which was distortion of the pressure vessel liner. This meant that the boilers could not be installed between the reactor and pressure vessel. Accordingly, the liner had to be dismantled and rebuilt. Although this led to additional expenditure of £200,000, the real cost was in terms of the resulting 18-month delay.

The problems did not end there, with boiler design deficiencies necessitating significant modifications. The cumulative effect was that, in 1969 – with work well behind schedule – APC went into administration. Project management was taken over by the CEGB, who appointed British Nuclear Design and Construction (BNDC) as the new main contractor. This did not, unfortunately, prove to be in any way a panacea. By 1971, Dungeness A was suffering from corrosion of mild steel components, which gave designers cause for further concern – because the Dungeness B restraint couplings were of the same material. As a preventative measure, it was decided to replace these components. The following year – two years after the original planned completion date – more problems were discovered within the galvanised wire used to attach thermocouples to the stainless-steel boiler tubes. At this stage, a new estimate put costs rising to £170 million. By 1975, the CEGB was advising that the completion date had slipped to 1977, with costs now anticipated to top £280 million. Yet this was still not the end of the matter: by 1979, work was still ongoing, and cost estimates had reached £410 million. When reactor one eventually started generating power on 3 April 1983, the project was 13 years behind schedule and had cost £685 million,[3] four times the initial estimate. The second reactor came into use two years later, in 1985.

Dungeness A reached the end of its life and ceased generation on 31 December 2006. The long process of defueling took until June 2012, with demolition of the turbine hall completed in June 2015. This is not the end of the story, however, as nuclear power regulations require a very long decommissioning process and Dungeness A is not due to enter the care and maintenance stage until 2027. Following privatisation of the electricity supply industry and subsequent part-privatisation of the nuclear power industry, the two power stations are rather perversely now owned by two different bodies: the original Magnox plant Dungeness A by the non-departmental government body, the Nuclear Decommissioning Authority (NDA) and Dungeness B by French company EDF,[4] through its British subsidiary, EDF Energy.

Dungeness B has continued to be plagued by problems, with routine maintenance in March 2009 identifying serious problems within reactor one – resulting in it having to be shut

The power stations and their infrastructure: a familiar view from the top of the old lighthouse (2017)

---

3. Cost estimates have been adjusted to allow for inflation during the construction period.
4. Electricité de France.

down for 18 months. Just eight months later, a fire resulted in the second reactor also being closed down. Since then, further unplanned shutdowns have been necessary on a number of occasions. In 2005, what is formally known as the station's accounting closure date was set for 2018, giving it a lifespan of 35 years. In 2015, however, the plant was awarded a ten-year life extension, necessitating an upgrade to the control room computer systems.

Operations

There are two safety requirements that are worthy of discussion. The first of these is the need for abundant supplies of water, the raison d'être for power stations being sited at Dungeness. Up to 100 million litres of water are extracted from the sea each hour, to cool the wet steam from the turbines. This process converts the steam into water, which is circulated back into the boilers to prevent the unimaginable consequences of overheating.

A result of this is that the same volume of hot water, as well as other waste from the power station, is pumped back into the sea through two outfall pipes. At the point that this enters the sea its temperature is some 12°C higher than the surrounding water, and it has been claimed that this has resulted in the creation of a discrete marine microclimate. Certainly, the area attracts all manner of marine and bird life, all the way up the food chain: many different fish will be found in this area; and there is also an established sea bass nursery in the vicinity. The re-entry point is widely known as "the outfall", "the patch" or, to anglers – for reasons which will be quite obvious when observed – "the boil".

Research, however, suggests that this hotter water is cooled so quickly on its return to the sea that the impact is minimal. What is far more significant is that fish that have been sucked into the pipes but managed to avoid the filters inevitably die before progressing through the

The frenzied activity of seabirds leaves no doubt as to the point at which water and waste products from the power station return to the sea

cooling process. Although nuclear protocols preclude these fish being returned whole direct to the sea and the food chain, they do allow their return after undergoing maceration. This return is via the same outfall pipes, which means that "the patch" is fed with rich nutrients and it is this that attracts the bulk of the sea and birdlife. There is no reliable evidence of genetically modified fish stocks – or even two-headed fish – resulting from nuclear activity, as claimed by some of the more sensationalist tabloid newspapers.

Inevitably, there are times when the quantity of fish in the vicinity of the intake pipes causes operational difficulty. This is particularly the case when shoals of sprats are in abundance, and filter screens sometimes become blocked, which has resulted in reactors being shut down on a number of occasions – with financial consequences. A similar situation has arisen from time to time in relation to floating seaweed.

One of the main risks associated with the generation of nuclear energy is clearly that of radiation, or radioactive leakage. Ongoing monitoring is undertaken, by both the nuclear industry and the Environment Agency, to provide reassurance to the public. In addition to the regular extraction of borehole samples for analysis, some lower-tech techniques are also utilised. This picture shows one of a number of what locals (with black humour) term "gallows trees", from which are suspended fine mesh socks. These collect any radioactive particles present in the environment; these are then analysed by power station scientists. The testing takes place at the Dungeness B District Survey Laboratory, situated next to the approach road, which also holds low activity radioactive sources for the purposes of calibrating detection instruments. From time to time, the media does report scare stories, such as the discovery (from routine borehole tests) of traces of tritium – which can increase the risk of cancer – measuring more than seven times the agreed level. Tritium, however, is generally considered to be one of the least dangerous of nuclear waste products and, in reality, there are higher levels of naturally occurring radioactivity within rocks in Cornwall than have so far been recorded in proximity to the Dungeness power stations.

The nature of the nuclear industry is such that there is ongoing reappraisal of risk, no more so than following major incidents. One such was the Fukushima disaster of March 2011, when a tsunami resulting from the Tohuku earthquake disabled the emergency generators that provided power to operate pumps required to cool the reactors. This led to three nuclear meltdowns, and the release of radioactive material. In its wake, new world-wide regulations were put in place, which necessitated the construction of a new flood wall at Dungeness in March 2014 – and the shutdown of the reactor for five months whilst this was undertaken. The circumstances were not made public at the time, with the result that, when discovered by

Nanny Goat Island

The flood wall around Dungeness B now offers an additional line of defence against the sea

the media the following year, there were accusations of a cover-up. At the start of 2015, thousands of tons of rocks and boulders were imported from Scandinavia to form a barrier to provide a further line of sea defence.

The shingle problem

There is an ongoing need to physically move shingle around the coast to counter the threat of the power stations being undermined, as already identified. This, in itself, is not an action devoid of consequences and has frequently brought the power station owners into conflict with the community; gestures such as allowing local residents to use the access road only go so far in terms of goodwill. The main issue has been where the bulldozing of shingle has altered the profile of the beach, preventing fishermen from launching off the east beach. This became a particular problem in January 2001, when many boats were unable to put to sea for a number of weeks. Things came to a head when the fishing community formed a human blockade across the power station access road and the dispute was only resolved with the intervention of local MP Michael Howard. Nowadays, matters are handled much more diplomatically, with ongoing dialogue involving all interested parties.

Cross Channel Converter

From an early stage, Dungeness additionally hosted the first HVDC (High Voltage Direct Current) Cross-Channel converter. This ran under the channel and linked the British and continental Europe electricity grids. It was bi-directional, allowing France and Britain to import or export electricity in accordance with market demand. It was completed in 1961, in advance of Dungeness A, but became obsolete in 1984 when replaced by a more powerful inverter constructed at nearby Sellindge. The long, low building to the west of Dungeness B, which connects to the national grid, also provides the link to Sellindge.

8. Going Nuclear – The Dungeness Power Stations

The National Grid's Dungeness Step-Up transformer connects to the national grid

Electricity Link Station

The "switch" connecting and disconnecting the electricity grids of Britain and France was formerly provided by the Electricity Link Station, at the northern end of Dungeness village. This building was completed in 1957, ahead of the Converter Station, and was both lined with, and surrounded by, copper earthing.

The Link House was put on the market in 2014, although there were some restrictive conditions placed on its future use. Some of these have since been lifted and the building – now privately owned – has been renamed On a Way. Estate regulations preclude it being used as a primary residence, and at the time of writing it remains unoccupied.

The former Link House, sited close to the RHDR line and the Pilot public house

Dungeness C?

Since the early 1970s, rumours of a third power station have been rife. By 1978, when a new position was proposed to the north of the existing site – with its perimeter fence very close to a number of cottages and near to The Pilot public house – the local populace was up in arms. In the end, it was discovery of a possible seismic fault under the proposed site that resulted in abandonment of the scheme. Further plans drawn up in 1987 also came to nothing, but by now protest was more organised than it had been in 1960, with numerous public interest groups combining with the Dungeness Leaseholders Association to form the Save Our Dungeness Official Fighting Force. This deserved to succeed, if only for its memorable acronym (SODOFF)!

In 2007, Dungeness was included in a short list of eight; and then again, in April 2009 – at the request of EDF Energy – as one of 11 potential sites for new nuclear power stations. But it did not make it onto the government shortlist published in its draft National Policy Statement later that year, owing to concerns over coastal erosion presenting an enhanced flood risk. Proponents have cited the fact that new technology, which has resulted in the development of smaller reactor types, could well suit the Dungeness site. It is ironic, giving the previous opposition to nuclear power at Dungeness, that a third power station now has the backing of the bulk of the community – which even organised a petition demanding that the government elevate it to the shortlist. Damien Collins, Folkestone & Hythe MP, has also consistently lobbied Parliament to reconsider. Clearly, the economic benefits of nuclear power have now been recognised, even if safety concerns persist. Dungeness B currently employs 750 staff, some 75% of all those working within a 15-mile radius. And, at times of planned maintenance, the need to bring in specialist workers can increase this number by up to 1200, which provides a further boost to the local economy.

9

For the Birds (and Other Species) – A Special Place for Nature

Statutory protection

The need to preserve land of significance for scientific, landscape and cultural, as well as wildlife, reasons was recognised very early in the 20th century by the Society for the Promotion of Nature Reserves.[1] The Society produced a first list of such sites in 1915 and this included Dungeness. Today, there are numerous different levels of protection that may be bestowed and Dungeness has been awarded what may be regarded as "the full set", including: Site of Special Scientific Interest (SSSI), Special Protection Area (SPA[2]) and Special Area of Conservation (SAC) status.[3] Each requires special attention to be paid to the preservation and protection of the environment, and the SSSI legislation, for example, prescribes fines of up to £25k for intentional or reckless destruction, damage or disturbance to the flora, fauna or shingle ridges.

One of Dungeness' most important designations is that of a National Nature Reserve (NNR), considered to be the crown jewel of English Nature's conservation strategy. Although the prime function of such sites is to offer protection to wildlife, they must also contribute to the Government's international and national priorities for nature conservation, maintain and develop practical experience of land management for nature conservation, and provide access for the enjoyment of England's wildlife and heritage.[4] The Dungeness NNR, which incorporates parts of Lydd-on-Sea and Greatstone, is the most visited in the country, as well as one of the most expensive to run.

There are numerous stakeholders who work together both to ensure compliance with legislation and to look after the best interests of wildlife. These include the Romney Marsh Countryside Partnership, which was established in June 1996 to "care for the special landscape and wildlife of the Romney Marsh and Dungeness". Estate owners EDF are also involved, but two of the main bodies – the Royal Society for the Protection of Birds (RSPB) and the

---

1. An organisation that, following numerous name changes, still exists – now as the Royal Society of Wildlife Trusts.
2. Specific to bird habitats.
3. Generally, the names and acronyms of some of these bodies have changed over time.
4. A current concern – and potential threat to wildlife – is that the bulk of this legislation has been driven by European directives. In the post-Brexit drive to de-regulate, the risk is that wildlife protection in these and other designated sites is likely to suffer.

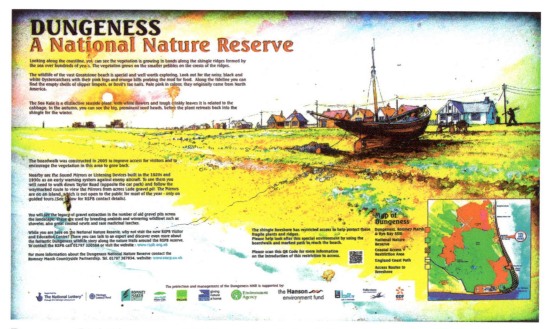

Dungeness Bird Observatory (DBO) – quite obviously have the interests of birdlife at their core. This is understandable, given that its geographical location makes Dungeness one of the country's most important sites for migrating birds. Accordingly, many initiatives have been undertaken to preserve and manage the landscape to attract and accommodate breeding birds. However, some measures aimed at achieving this end can impact upon other wildlife. This can be positive – particularly in terms of insect and amphibian populations for example – but can reduce the food source for other species, such as foxes and badgers. It is a very delicate balancing act but, thankfully, in recent years the RSPB has acknowledged that, owning such large areas of diverse habitats, it has an obligation to consider all kinds of wildlife – because maintaining a healthy ecosystem brings benefits to all species within it. One major initiative to have involved Dungeness in recent years has been the re-introduction of the short-haired bumblebee, as discussed within Chapter 1. In addition to also being home to the great crested newt, the medicinal leech and the marsh frog, insect species of particular interest include the brown-tailed moth, marsh mallow moth, emperor dragonfly, Sussex emerald moth, pigmy footman moth, grizzled skipper butterfly and great silver water beetle.

Royal Society for the Protection of Birds (RSPB)

It is widely reported that Dungeness was the RSPB's first reserve. This is incorrect: strangely, that accolade belongs to another site on Romney Marsh, the nearby Cheyne Court (current home to the controversial wind farm). This 18-acre meadow was purchased in 1928, but was sold in 1950 after drainage modifications to the Marsh resulted in it losing its attraction for

9. For the Birds (and other species) – A Special Place for Nature

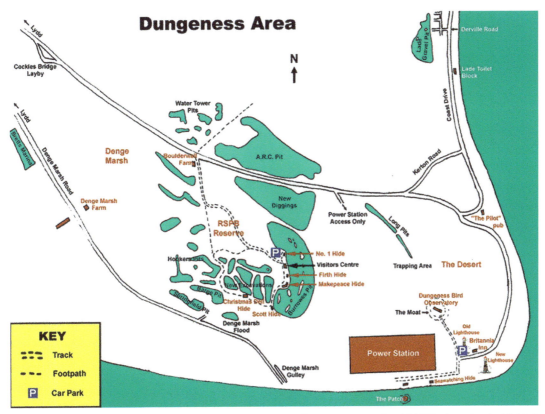

Map showing the gravel pits and the RSPB and BDO presence at Dungeness, as at the mid-1990s (reproduced with kind permission of southeastbirdnews.co.uk). Whilst some further gravel extraction has taken place, the map remains quite representative

birdlife. In 1931, the organisation purchased land at two further sites, of which Dungeness was one – although it was another two years before they were to make a formal announcement to this effect. It does, nonetheless, make Dungeness the joint oldest of the RSPB's current reserves.

The story actually begins some time before this. In 1908, the fledgling RSPB appointed two "watchers" – Fred Austen and John ("Jack") Tart – at Dungeness. This was considered necessary because of both the growing popularity of the collection of birds' eggs and public ignorance of how their activities could affect nesting birds. One of these watchers was deputed to guard the seabird colonies, whilst the other was tasked with protecting nesting beach birds (specifically the Kentish plover and the stone curlew). But the embryonic organisation had not yet developed the wider influence that it would later achieve and it had no effective means of appealing against the siting of the RH&DR line on prime nesting land in 1928. The fact that Kentish plovers stopped breeding at Dungeness after 1930 can be attributed to the building of the light railway and gravel excavation operations rather than the actions of selfish or misguided individuals.

Nanny Goat Island

In 1929, Richard Burrowes[5] – whose name would become inextricably linked to the area – bought Boulderwall Farm, along with 50 acres of land adjoining the Lydd–Dungeness Road. Burrowes was a great lover of nature and had seen just how important this unique habitat was to so many species of birdlife. He was a familiar figure in the area, although considered to be a little eccentric, spending much of his time patrolling the shingle on his bike (no mean feat in itself). He used an old-fashioned horn to try to deter anyone he suspected of being an egg collector, earning himself the nickname "Seagull Pete". He was also an RSPCA council member, and it was only some 18 months later that he made the first of a number of substantial personal donations to the RSPB, to enable them to make a start on developing a reserve. Their first purchase involved the 250-acre area known as Walkers Outlands.[6] The rest of the reserve would be acquired piecemeal, but there was a major purchase in 1935, which included the Oppen Pits. When Richard Burrowes died in 1956, at the age of 85, he would bequeath his earlier private purchases, including Boulderwall Farm, to the Society.[7]

The RSPB reserve has continued to grow in size over the years and now incorporates the ARC pit – just across the Lydd–Dungeness Road, with vehicular access from opposite Boulderwall Farm. This is the result of co-operation with the aggregates company, which handed over the site on completion of its gravel extraction work. In December 2015, the RSPB also acquired Lade Pits (Greatstone Lakes), after Cemex had completed 15 years of quarrying the site. The reserve now occupies nearly 1000 hectares (four square miles).

In 1940, the reserve was requisitioned by the army for use as a gunnery training range. Interestingly, tank tracks from this time can still be seen on the shingle, demonstrating the vulnerability of this landscape. By the time the majority of the reserve was returned to the

Boulderwall Farm (left) at the entrance to the RSPB Reserve; and the RSPB Visitor Centre (right) (both 2018)

5. Frequently incorrectly spelt "Burrows".
6. This is an unremarkable patch of shingle and scrub, still marked on maps. It is just to the east of the RSPB access road.
7. This was in spite of a major falling out, when the RSPB decided to sell off Cheyne Court – a move that Burrowes strongly opposed.

9. For the Birds (and other species) – A Special Place for Nature

The Oppen Pits (left) are within the RSPB reserve, about half a mile north east of the Dungeness power station, close to the south-eastern side of the Burrowes Pit. They are accessible by footpath and comprise two separate ponds, each originally the size of two football pitches – but now seemingly smaller owing to the growth of reeds and the encroachment of willow. This vegetation meant that, in summer months, they were until recently only clearly visible from the air or on maps; but the southern pit was cleared in 2017/18 (right)

Society 12 years later, very few of the seabird colonies remained.[8] There was now, however, a new threat – the growth of the fox population. Attracted by the vast numbers of rabbits then present at Dungeness, they were also ravaging the eggs and nests of the many species of ground-nesting birds that frequented the reserve. In response, Herbert Axell, the new RSPB warden, conceived what was, for then, the fairly revolutionary idea of constructing lakes with islands to offer the birds a measure of protection.[9]

Axell's idea was not taken up straight away, but was given fresh impetus when, at nearby Rye Harbour, gulls and terns started to nest and breed successfully on the islands left in flooded but unmanaged gravel pits. Work on the most important of the Dungeness reserve's lakes did not begin until 1970 and took eight years to complete. This is the stretch of water alongside the Visitor Centre, which was fittingly named the Burrowes Pit. It has since been extended and re-modelled a number of times.

The announcement of planning consent to the building of Dungeness A in 1958 caused great consternation, as it involved a large area of undisturbed shingle that was important for many seabird colonies. Whilst it cannot be denied that this was a significant setback to birdlife, the construction and power companies have since worked together to manage the impact on the environment. There have even been some unexpected benefits, with the large structure of the power stations providing an unusual but safe nesting site for birds such as the black redstart.

---

8. One RSPB historian has recorded that: "all the sea bird colonies were disturbed to extinction".
9. At this time there was no open water at Dungeness, with the exception of the Oppen Pits.

Nanny Goat Island

The Burrowes Pit, 2015 – now home to half the population of the endangered Mediterranean Gull as well as many other species – as seen from the RSPB Visitor Centre

As to be expected, the RSPB reserve is now visitor-friendly, but with the delicate balance between the needs of man and wildlife well maintained. There is a two-mile circular nature trail, which keeps visitors away from breeding sites and can accommodate both wheelchair users and pushchairs. Along the main trail are six hides. A new state-of-the art visitor centre was built in 1991, which has stunning views over the Burrowes Pit.

Dungeness Bird Observatory (DBO)

The other body to champion the interests of birds here is the Dungeness Bird Observatory (DBO). It is also a registered charity, operated by an independent Board of Trustees. Its original aim was to study migration patterns, through both observation and ringing, and these practices continue today – offering an insight into future habitat management.

The DBO has its origins in a meeting held in the RH&DR light railway café in March 1952, convened by the Kent Ornithological Society (KOS). It involved representatives of various other conservation bodies, one of which was the RSPB. Mr Denby Wilkinson, on behalf of a special Dungeness Committee of the Hastings Natural History Society, advised that he had been in conversation with Mr Gordon T Paine, the mayor of Lydd, who had just purchased the Dungeness Estate from British Rail.[10] Paine had indicated that he wished to preserve the estate in its current state, and that he would approve a bird observatory operating from it. To this end, it was agreed to work towards establishing such a facility by the autumn; and to build a first trap for the purpose of ringing.

With funding from a number of sources, including both the RSPB and the Nature Conservancy, accommodation was secured initially through the rental of the first floor of the Watch House on the old RNSSS site. Eleven months later, in May 1953, the DBO transferred to No.

---

10. See Chapter 11.

9. For the Birds (and other species) – A Special Place for Nature

The DBO accommodation building, in use in March 2018

11 Quarter, the end-of-row cottage in the same block. Because of concerns over how renting the property to an organisation might be perceived when there was such a shortage of residential accommodation, the Admiralty Surveyor insisted that the DBO secretary be shown as the nominal tenant.

Ringing was, and remains, the main raison d'être for the DBO, and requires the use of traps and nets. There has been a succession of different traps used over the years, many of which have been of the impressive Heligoland[11] variety. The effectiveness of these has reduced over time, however, because the increasingly drier conditions have allowed the salix (willow) plants to thrive. These can form dense and impenetrable "jungle" which unfortunately obstructs hide entrances and discourages birds. Some of the obsolete traps have been allowed to rot away which, to an extent, complements the natural decay of the nearby fishing beach. Most of the nets in use today are of the "mist" variety, which can be stored discreetly *in situ* when not in use. Yet care still has to be taken with their placement, for the salix plants often interfere with their efficiency, too.

In order to place nets and traps, the permission of the landowner is required, and the DBO is a licensee of that part of the estate on which it operates. The licence was originally granted at no cost by GT Paine and, subsequently, the trustees instituted a peppercorn rent, which was continued by the new owner (Hall Aggregates [South East] Ltd) when that part of the estate was sold in 1986. These arrangements have remained in operation, first under licence from Cemex (which absorbed Hall Aggregates) and – since 2013, when the lakes were further sold on – from EDF Energy.

---

11. Named after the German North Sea archipelago, where this type of trap was first used. Its great advantage is that it can be used in any weather conditions.

A Heligoland trap, still in use in 2018. It is located just outside the redoubt, in an area known as The Moat

Birds humanely trapped in these devices are placed into cloth bags and taken away for ringing. This activity was originally carried out in the field, with birds only occasionally being brought back to the Watch House. When the observatory moved to its new premises, however, the front room was allocated for the task, with ringed birds being released through its window. It was not until 1981 that the first ringing hut was built and installed in the garden. This was replaced ten years later.

The DBO has a resident warden, and an assistant in place for much of the year. A Central Electricity Generating Board (CEGB) initiative provided an annual grant towards the cost of

Two smaller and simpler traps – no longer used – in the Trapping Area (pictured in 2014)

9. For the Birds (and other species) – A Special Place for Nature

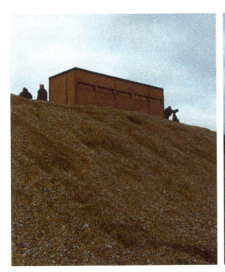 

The Seawatch Hide (left) and more substantial Patch Hide (right) (both pictured in 2018). Note the size of the shingle bank, which offers a measure of protection to the power station buildings against the power of the sea

employing the warden,[12] starting in 1959, and its costs are still part-funded by the companies running the power station, as part of community programmes. Further funding is provided by the Friends of Dungeness and paying contributions also come from guests and visiting volunteers staying on site. Those who do stay on site may use the two hides located on Dungeness beach (the keys to which are held at the observatory).

The Patch Hide – directly opposite the power station water outlet, and financed by the CEGB – was the first of these to be constructed, in 1975. This proved to be so popular that it was sometimes difficult to get in! Accordingly, in 1986, the DBO considered extending it, but abandoned this plan when the CEGB offered to build another. This, the Seawatch Hide, opened in September 1987. The timing was particularly unfortunate, as it was only a few short weeks before the most violent hurricane to strike Britain in generations. Dungeness did not escape, and both hides were reduced to matchwood. CEGB's generosity persisted, however, and the organisation funded two replacements, which were handed over to the DBO in February 1989.

A new problem manifested itself in 1996, when a combination of longshore drift and the artificial movement of shingle to protect the power station changed the beach profile to such an extent that visibility from the Patch Hide was greatly impaired. CEGB again stepped in to move and raise the hide, although this work was not completed until 1998. The hide remained *in situ* until replaced again, after a further storm did its worst.

In common with the RSPB, the DBO has extended its remit in recent years and its activities now include the study and recording of butterflies, moths, insects and local flora and fungi.

---

12. As the warden served the interests of both the observatory and the RSPB, this grant has been administered by the latter.

Nanny Goat Island

The Long Pits

There are two further bodies of water in the area which, despite not having the same importance as those on the RSPB reserve, nonetheless have some significance for birds and other wildlife. These are the Long Pits, comprising former gravel workings sited to the north of Dungeness. They sit alongside the Dungeness–Lydd road, and extend southwards. Taken over by EDF Energy from an aggregates company, they have at no time been under either RSPB or DBO administration. Nevertheless, the DBO trapping area extends as far as the Long Pits, and in 1978 a hide overlooking the water was erected in memory of their long-standing committee member Dick Holmes. This, however, saw very little use and was subject to vandalism. What little remained was removed in 1993 and not replaced.

At times, the Long Pits attract interesting species of migrant birds, and their more remote location (in comparison with other lakes in the area) often means that they hold birds later in the day. The waters are rich with leeches, frogs and fish (with day tickets being available for the purpose of fishing). As part of an initiative by EDF Energy, the pits were awarded the Wildlife Trust's Biodiversity Benchmark, following an audit at the end of 2017.[13]

The Long Pits, looking south from the Lydd–Dungeness road end (2018)

---

13. Bringing the area in line with the rest of the EDF Energy landholding around the power station site.

10

Serving the Public – Amenities and Services

For those visiting Dungeness for the first time, the thought that the village has ever offered much in the way of amenities may be quite fanciful. Certainly, as already established, the village was very late to receive a service road, and even later to have mains water laid on. This was ironic, given the presence of the water tower at Dengemarsh, which, prior to the building of the power stations, had for long dominated the local landscape.

Electricity did not arrive until 1961 and, prior to this time, households mostly made use of small pot-bellied multi-fuel heaters (which later gave way to gas and paraffin stoves). Light was obtained either from candle-power, paraffin lamps or pressure lamps – which were in turn sometimes adapted for the purpose of heating water. Mains drainage still remains a dream, however, meaning that cess tanks must still be emptied on a regular basis – although, in fairness, there are numerous other communities in the same boat.

Despite these limiting factors, those more in tune with the local culture will realise that the residents of Dungeness have always been very adaptable and imaginative in ensuring not only that the community has survived, but that it has thrived. In particular, numerous pubs and cafés/tea rooms have flourished over the years, and the village also boasted its own school for more than 60 years.

The Dengemarsh Water tower was built in 1902 for the Littlestone & District Water Company, to provide water for New Romney, Littlestone, Greatstone and Lydd, and employed many local men. Its distinctive red top was visible for miles around but was replaced in the 1960s with the white and larger concrete cap that can be seen today (right)

Education

Dungeness School

Local histories have it that Dungeness School ("The School Beautiful"), built to the seaward side of the old railway track (just to the north of the current Polish Airmen memorial), was founded in 1876. Records of a Diocesan Education Society donation, however, suggest that it was more likely to have been the following year. The landowners donated the site to the vicar and churchwardens of Lydd for a Church of England (CoE) school, but, in 1906, responsibility for its running was taken over by the Kent Education Authority. Its use was not confined to education: it also operated as a chapel (with an altar behind the east window in an area curtained off when the school was in use) and as a Sunday School – with regular outings to Greatstone on the RH&DR for its pupils. For a time, it was also used as a community centre.

The school badge was a most distinctive shield depicting a black and white lighthouse with beams of light radiating out on a yellow background and the inscription "Play the Game". The school probably reflected the characteristics of many such village institutions of an era long gone, and would have given any of today's OFSTED inspectors a heart attack. At play-time or other breaks, children were given free rein and would be allowed to roam the 'Ness and explore its ponds with limited or no supervision.

The Old School House, pictured between the wars

Much interesting research into the school has been undertaken by two brothers – Edwin and Harry Cawkell. The former (a journalist) discovered a document relating to the school year ending May 1883, which recorded that the population of Dungeness was "less than 200 souls", and the school roll just 39 (of which boys comprised 24). Five of the pupils were three years of age and two were only a year older. One was over 14 and there were few others over 12 – reflecting that, in a fishing community, children were often expected to contribute to the family income from an early age. Attendance was poor, with a highest weekly average over the academic year of 22. Parents were required to contribute two old pence per week per child towards the cost of their education, which was considered by the education authorities to be: "fairly within the means of a common labouring man in the neighbourhood".[1] At the time, managers were required to test the accuracy of class registers, but it is noteworthy that nobody had visited the Dungeness school within the previous academic year. This was because the managers were resident in Lydd and New Romney, demonstrating that Dungeness was still considered to be, for many, literally a step too far.

At this time, too, there was just the one classroom, which was 33 feet in length by 18 feet wide,[2] but other rooms would later be added.[3] There was seemingly only the one formal teaching role, with the post being filled by Jane Richards. It is a shame that her initial impressions were not recorded, for they would surely have made great reading. She lacked formal qualifications and it seems that she failed to produce the required testimonial of her moral and intellectual fitness. It is tempting to wonder just how many others applied for the post, and it appears that Miss Richards may even have been appointed through correspondence without ever having visited the village. When she took up the post, she was 26 years of age and had spent her whole adult life teaching in East London. The contrast must have been enormous. At this point, though, the accounts of the Cawkell brothers diverge. Edwin writes that Jane Richards spent the rest of her working life at the school and was remembered by all whom she taught, although her strict nature meant that this was often out of respect rather than affection; and that she remained in the village when she retired.

In contrast, Harry Cawkell suggests that Miss Richards only taught at the school for two years, later (on her retirement) returning to live out the rest of her days at Dungeness – dying shortly before the end of WWII, just short of her ninetieth birthday. It is this (Harry's) account that is supported by official records, which show her as headteacher between 1883–85.[4] The same source shows her being succeeded by Miss Bowrick (1885–1889); Miss Stevens (1889–1890); Miss Abernethy 1890–1892; Miss Marsh (1892–1908); Miss Fox (1908–

---

1. This was a generalisation which may have applied to some more affluent areas, but not to many residents of Dungeness.
2. The document also shows it to have been 18 feet high which, if correct, is quite remarkable.
3. Although no dates can be confirmed, it seems that this was post-1929.
4. It is possible that Miss Richards did additionally serve as an assistant after the appointment of a more qualified headteacher. It may be safely inferred that she grew to love Dungeness.

Nanny Goat Island

1925);[5] and Miss Lexie Bottle serving the final term (1936–1940).[6] Other narratives, though, refer to a Miss Wilman being headteacher in the 1920s, with a Miss Ovenden working to her and a senior girl, Mabel Lusted,[7] taken on to teach the infants (at a rate of £1 a month). The reality is that Miss Wilman was probably a teacher under Miss Fox, and that at this time the school was much better staffed than most, given the low roll.

The roll never totalled much above 60 and, by the outbreak of WWII, was down to around 30. These numbers did not allow anything more than a generic split by age group so, for the most part, the younger children from 5 to 11 were taught in one room and the older children (up to the school leaving age of 14) in another. It didn't allow for great learning

The School Beautiful, post-WWII, showing the ravages of vandalism and neglect (photo, left, courtesy Mike Golding). The site is now denoted by some faint remains of the foundations and a wild rose bush. It is not possible to verify the claim that this was planted by a member of staff and was the only plant to grow in the grounds

5. Subsequently Mrs Stevenson, after she married for the second time (her new husband being the landlord of the George Hotel, Lydd).
6. An often-told story is that, on her arrival, Miss Bottle was invited by the keeper to admire the view from the top of the lighthouse. She noticed that three main paths radiated out from the schoolhouse, presumably created by her predecessors. She was appalled to learn that one led to The Pilot Inn, another to the Britannia and the other to the (only recently defunct) Hope & Anchor pub!
7. This is the same Mabel Lusted whose account of life as one of the early railway carriage dwellers is recounted in Chapter 7.

opportunities either, although the curriculum included the staples of maths, English, scripture, geography and history. Other lessons were provided in gardening, country dancing, keep fit, singing (including sea shanties and folk songs), drama and (demonstrating the growing importance of radio technology to many families on the 'Ness), wireless study. There was also a strong emphasis on nature studies, and spending time in the great outdoors. Anecdotally, from the age of nine or ten, girls were required to clean staff quarters and even cook for the adults, under the guise of what would later be called domestic science!

What the school did offer was a happy environment and a level of integration that was lacking elsewhere within the community. The fishing families and those at the other end of the village involved with Trinity House, the Admiralty and Coastguard rarely mingled. Indeed, many parents forbade their children from mixing. This was also subsequently (from the 1920s) the case with the incoming railway families (those that chose to make their permanent home here). Whilst the underlying tensions may have never been fully addressed, the school provided a means for future generations to put prejudices aside. The school motto was: "Kindness, honesty and helping to play the game", displayed on a board in the main hall, and the teachers promoted a strong moral code. If any child committed a major misdemeanour – such as stealing – this motto board would be turned to face the wall. But there was compassion, too, with those children living at Pen Bars and facing a long walk home being allowed to leave early in the winter months.

Up until the outbreak of WWII, it had been the proud boast of the school that it had only ever closed for a very brief period (in 1896), owing to a measles outbreak. But, following Dungeness being declared a restricted area, most children were evacuated,[8] and its life came to a premature end in 1940. The school was requisitioned by the army and those few children who did remain were taught by a Miss Penny in a nearby house (half a mile down the track, just beyond the old Pilot Inn).[9] By the time that hostilities had come to an end, the school building had been damaged to such an extent that it was decided that it would not be reopened, with the Dungeness children instead being assigned to Lydd School. To start with, most would have to walk – a round trip of over six miles – although, subsequently, taxis would be laid on. Interestingly, there was still an unofficial segregation here, with separate taxis used for the fishing families in the north of the village (the "top-enders") and the incomers ("bottom-enders") to the south. Children from both parts of the village reported that their Lydd counterparts were unfriendly towards them, with the tag "Nanny Goat Islanders" often being used with derision.

In 1952, whilst it was still in the hands of the Kent Education Committee, the newly-formed Dungeness Bird Observatory briefly had designs on taking over the old school building. But, in the intervening years, the fabric had deteriorated even further, to the extent that a

---

8. The majority to villages in West Sussex. Some families could not adjust to separation, however, and soon recalled their children.
9. A property that went by the name of Foam.

survey deemed such a move to be unviable.[10] Accordingly, instead of the building being given a new lease of life, nature was allowed to take its course. By the mid-1960s it had almost completely decayed, although rubble from the foundations can still be found if you know where to look. A more lasting tribute is the school song, written by teacher Miss Lillian Wilman in the 1920s:

> Away by the sea where God's air blows free,
> Surrounded by beach and by stone,
> Stands a quaint little school,
> The school that we love and one we are proud to own;
> The school, the school beautiful,[11]
> The school we are proud to claim,
> That teaches us through shine and shower
> Always to play the game.

The school also features prominently in the 1951 Malcolm Saville book, *The Elusive Grasshopper*.[12]

Library services

Whilst library services have traditionally been a part of local authorities' education and learning policies, small communities such as Dungeness have not always been well served. As described at Chapter 6, a small lending library operated from the fourth lighthouse during WWII. In addition to this, a similar facility was one of the many services run from Spion Kop at one time.

Worship

In places as isolated as Dungeness, arrangements for religious meetings have also often been *ad hoc*. As this was a fishing community, it is highly likely that regular worship would have taken place from early times, and the claim of there being a 16th century chapel dedicated to St Mary here is quite in keeping. The third lighthouse, built in 1792, had its own chapel, although whether this was installed at the outset or added later – and whether this was for lighthouse personnel only – is yet another area open to conjecture. The redoubt, batteries Nos

---

10. This survey found jackdaws, little owls and stock doves all to be in residence within the building.
11. Whether it was this song that led to the school's nickname, or that it had been coined before, is unknown.
12. Part of Saville's Lone Pine saga, which references many locations in the Rye and Romney Marsh area.

10. Serving the Public – Amenities and Services

1, 3 and 4, Coastguard Station and Signal Station were all pressed into use for religious services at various times, too.

The establishment of the school allowed for some more permanent arrangements to be instigated, as described above. Details of the clergy performing services are unknown prior to December 1885, but, at that time, young Joseph Castle became assistant curate at Lydd. He took his duties as "Curate to the Coast" very seriously,[13] and the timing of his appointment, just two years after Dungeness Station opened to passenger traffic, undoubtedly helped him in his cause; although there was no Sunday train service, the curate was able to travel along the track on the workmen's trolley.

This simple pump trolley was designed to accommodate three men, and two Lydd residents would regularly volunteer to accompany Castle. Accordingly, he was able to literally take a back seat and arrive at Dungeness in a relaxed state. On arrival, he would then have to walk to whichever venue was hosting the day's service. The same arrangements remained in place for Castle's successor, when he left the area in 1889.

Into the 20th century, the school came to be the most regular of the service venues. Post-WWII, with its deterioration and closure, a new site was sought. Temporary arrangements were put in place up until 1954, at which time a group of local residents (which included the lighthouse keeper) raised £300 for materials and undertook the work required to turn the end of a former PLUTO pumping station into a chapel, which became known as The Sanctuary. Dedicated for the celebration of Communion by the Archbishop of Canterbury, Dr Geoffrey Fisher, it sported a cross made from a broken skid taken from the lifeboat station and a bell donated by Trinity House.

The decision of the Trustees of the Dungeness Estate[14] to sell the Sanctuary building for private development in 2010 resulted in local uproar, but, post-renovation, it retains many of

The pump trolley used to transport the curate from Lydd to Dungeness. The clergyman in this photo from c. 1912 is not Joseph Castle, as he had left his post by this time. This is clearly a posed photograph, as the trolley could not have operated with a load of eight!

---

13. Castle's "patch" extended from Lade to Jury's Gap, and inland to Lydd. His life and times are recounted in the 1993 publication by Ted Carpenter and Margaret Bird: *Joseph Castle – Curate to the Coast*.
14. For details of administrative responsibilities of the Dungeness estate, see Chapter 11.

The Sanctuary, in religious use (top, mid-1950s); and post-conversion – with another former PLUTO building in the background (2017)

its earlier features – including the chapel-style windows on one of the side walls. Its sale means that most residents now have to travel to Greatstone or Lydd to satisfy their religious needs, although a Christmas Carol Service is now held at the Lifeboat Station.

In the 1960s, additional facilities for worship were provided for workers constructing Dungeness A power station, with the residential camp incorporating a dedicated chapel.

Leisure

For many fishing families, up until the end of WWII and for some good few years beyond, life was very much hand to mouth. Holidays were hardly ever taken, and even day trips were rare.

10. Serving the Public – Amenities and Services

Indeed, for many, the highlight of the year was a trek to Lydd to take in the annual Club Day. For the wives, this was the one occasion for which they might be able to expect a new outfit.

Predictably, angling and sailing competitions have formed the backbone of sporting activity at Dungeness down the years. These, at one time, included an annual regatta, which attracted fishing boats from Folkestone, Hythe and Rye as well as the Dungeness community. There has also been a strong interest (to use a rather outdated definition of the concept of sport) in hunting – particularly hare coursing. Tug-of-war, too, was taken very seriously at one time, with coastguard and lifeboat teams taking part – with some success – in local competitions.

It might be surmised that more "mainstream" sporting pursuits would have been limited by a lack of grass, but, in this respect, Dungeness yet again surprises. For example, a cricket club was formed in 1888. This was another brainchild of the inspirational Joseph Castle. Castle was a keen gardener and encouraged local families to develop their own gardens by importing top soil. This initiative met with only limited interest, but Castle had a greater vision and believed that a sports facility would improve the well-being and quality of life of many of the men. He thus petitioned the Commandant of the Coastguards for permission to lay a cricket pitch at the redoubt. This was achieved by digging mud from the beach at low tide and bringing in topsoil from Lydd. The cricket team comprised fishermen, lighthouse keepers and coastguards – a rare example of integration amongst the adults of the village. Although fairly short-lived, records show that the club was still functioning in 1895, hosting a number of matches with two innings per side. The facility was also made available to the

The Dungeness Snowflakes – the rather unlikely village football team – photographed sometime between 1908 and 1915. At this time, the majority of players were from the fishing community, but there are at least four coastguards/coastguard family members in this group

school and, in the winter months, converted to use for football. This activity was mainly limited to the schoolboys, although a group of older youths did establish a local team, the Dungeness Snowflakes, which played there for a number of years. The girls also partook of netball and stoolball here in the summer months.

In his time, Castle organised many other events and activities for the benefit of his flock. These included the establishment of a quoits league involving each of the coastguard/signal stations (at Dungeness, Dengemarsh [Pen Bars], Lydd and Jury's Gap). He was the driving force behind the annual regatta and also founded both a Dungeness Dramatic and Choral Society and a Children's Society for the provision of entertainment. Alongside all this, he had set up the first Buffalo Lodge (the RAOB) at Dungeness.[15]

Public houses

Given some of the hardships of life on the 'Ness during the 19th and early 20th centuries, it is hardly surprising that pubs have played a significant role in its history. Paul Copson, who was born and raised at Dungeness, is on record as saying that: "Dungeness was made up of a tremendously supportive community of hard-working people, sometimes hard drinking too!". More recently – at the time of construction of the power stations – a heightened demand for alcohol was driven by labourers; in the summer months quite a few would spend the night sleeping it off on the beach after too many hours in the local pubs.

There have been a disproportionate number of drinking establishments in the village, although we would struggle to recognise some of these in the context of today's pubs. All started out as beerhouses, run by fishermen to cater for the needs of themselves and neighbours. Most were part of a family home and some were little more than shacks on the shingle. Two long-gone establishments were the Jolly Sailor and the Dover Hoveller. Both are listed in a directory of 1818, and the former was sited (roughly) between the 1904 and 1961 lighthouses. Where the Dover Hoveller is concerned, it has always been assumed (based on crude maps of the time) that this was near to where the Old Boathouse now stands; however, recent research by local historian Linda Stanton suggests that it may rather have been to the north of Battery No. 1.

More is known of the Hope and Anchor, sited in the Pen Bars area at the end of Dengemarsh Road. This was a tarred and weatherboarded timber bungalow family home, but a large one, comprising four bedrooms and two living rooms. It was trading as a licensed house by 1847, and in 1879 was acquired by the Lydd Finn's Brewery. It had no dedicated bar area, but

---

15. This would appear to have been in appreciation of the RAOB having provided a lifeboat to the RNLI. For many years now, the RAOB has continued to support the Dungeness lifeboat service. This has not just been down to local efforts: in the 1970s, a former Lodge member moved from Lydd back to his native north London and encouraged his neighbouring Lodges to support his favourite cause – establishing a tradition that has continued.

10. Serving the Public – Amenities and Services

The British Sailor, c1936

was probably the largest of the beach pubs at this time, as it took in lodgers and was also used to hold inquests. In this regard, there is an interesting but sad historical footnote: at an inquest held here into the suicide of a woman in 1864, it was revealed that she had also killed her own baby. Her address was given as the same Hope & Anchor pub, and it seems that the hardship of living on the 'Ness with no regular income had resulted in her mental collapse. Confirming that this pub really was an integral part of the fishing community, one of its later landlords was fisherman Richard Tart. He took over the role in 1938 and was probably still in charge when the pub closed its doors for the last time in 1947.

Another pub in the vicinity was the British Sailor. This was not strictly part of Dungeness, sitting within the hamlet of Galloways. Yet it was used by many Dungeness families, and its roll of landlords includes the fishing names of Freathy and Oiller. Dating from around 1832 and (probably) originally a cottage for coastguards stationed here, by 1855 it was trading as a beerhouse. It closed in 1938, and was demolished by the army after wartime occupation.

There are two pubs, however, which have become synonymous with Dungeness over the years: The Pilot and the Britannia; and both can justifiably claim to have been at the heart of the community at various times. Both have existed on more than one site.

Britannia Inn

This also started life as a simple beerhouse, in 1850, when it was known for a time as the British Inn.[16] It was significantly to the north of the current site, and the location of the Britannia points on the RH&DR (the entry to its turning loop) is an accurate pointer to its

---

16. In the first edition of my book *Much Drinking in the Marsh*, I have wrongly implied that this name was used until the 1950s. Maps of the area show that the name "Britannia" was in official use at least from 1890, although it was for many years referred to by locals as simply *The Brit* and sometimes informally as the *Black Pig*.

The Britannia Inn in the 1930s (top – picture: courtesy Kent Messenger*). The Britannia, in May 2017 (below left), and with new sign (2019 – below right)*

former entity. In 1926, it was redesigned and rebuilt, mostly with corrugated iron. Soon after WWII, this ramshackle building burnt down. It was replaced by the curent brick building, constructed to the south, on the site of two former barrack rooms. The pub re-opened in 1955.

The Britannia has since had mixed fortunes, enjoying particularly good times in the 1970s and 80s. Struggling after this, it closed in 1992, soon after having changed its name to The Smugglers. On being sold, however, new owners re-opened it and restored goodwill by returning it to its former name and updating the décor. Since then, it has struggled to recapture its former glories, but new life was breathed into it with a major refurbishment in 2017/18. This indicates that its owners (brewers Shepherd Neame) feel that the increasing popularity of Dungeness as a destination is worth a substantial new investment. Indeed, the pub trades on its location as being the "only pub in Dungeness" (as The Pilot now sits just outside the Dungeness estate).

The Britannia has featured in a number of television programmes – most notably a 2006 episode of the Inspector Lindley detective series, and a 2007 instalment of the BBC soap opera, *EastEnders*.

The Pilot Inn

From the 17th century right up until 1957, The Pilot stood within the boundaries of Dungeness village. Now located right on its border in Lydd-on-Sea, it is probably only the owners of the Britannia who would argue against its village credentials. For, without doubt, within the annals of Dungeness, The Pilot has been the most influential of its public houses. Nevertheless, The Pilot has a very dark past. It seems that there was already a crude alehouse on the beach before, in 1633,[17] a three-masted frigate – the *Alfresia* – was lured onto the beach by wreckers. After murdering its crew, the wreckers looted the cargo of gold, wine and spirits, and even took the hold of the ship itself. This was then used to augment the structure of the pub.

The practices of wrecking and smuggling are often linked and the location of The Pilot made it inevitable that its clientele would also be involved in the latter. Over time, the pub came to incorporate features seen in other coastal pubs, such as sliding hatches from which smugglers could signal to boats at sea. Blockade officers were fully aware of what was taking place at The Pilot and fierce encounters took place here with the freetraders. Stakes were high and it is reported that, at one time, revenue officers were taken prisoner and lashed to tubs before being pushed out to sea and certain death. Others officers were shot, with their bodies buried nearby on the Lydd road.

Because the structure of some of these early Dungeness pubs was so basic and, there being no pressure on building land, when they became unserviceable there was no need to rebuild on the same site. Accordingly, new buildings were erected nearby and, when completed, licenses[18] would simply transfer with them. This explains why there is uncertainty about the history of some of the local establishments, and it is likely that The Pilot moved at least twice more before ending up at a spot close to the current entrance to the Dungeness estate. Pictures of it dating from around 1910 show a substantial timber building there, very similar in appearance to the Hope & Anchor at Pen Bars. For many years, it was run by members of the Tart fishing family.

For the early part of the 20th century, The Pilot tended to serve the fishing community (whereas the coastguard, signal station and lighthouse staff would use the Britannia, for social as well as locational reasons). During WWII, it was requisitioned by the army, and inevitably suffered some damage as a result. Yet things could have turned out so much worse: as reported in Chapter 3, in November 1943 a British aircraft returning from a mission dropped

---

17. This is not set in stone; some historians claim that this was a later date in the 17th century.
18. Even when there was a requirement to obtain a licence, not all alehouse owners would bother to apply, safe in the knowledge that there was little enforcement.

The old Pilot pub (top) was allowed to fall into decay after operations had moved to the current site (photo early 1960s; Chris Shore collection). The 1958 Pilot Inn (below) was very similar in design to the Britannia of the time

nine incendiary bombs on the beach, unaware that The Pilot was almost directly underneath. All its windows were destroyed but, fortunately, the building survived.

By 1957, the timber building was becoming badly weathered and deemed to be no longer repairable, so was replaced by a new modern structure. This was on the current site, just to the east of the RH&DR line, and the new pub opened in 1957/8.[19] A marketing drive was undertaken, with the owners rather imaginatively tapping into the area's wartime connections by adopting the slogan: Operation **P**atrons **L**ook **U**p **T**he **O**ld (PLUTO) Pilot Inn! The licensees, Reg and Ivy Turrell, were well liked and arranged a number of community events, including Friday night discos for the local teenagers.

---

19. October 1957 would seem to have been the date that the new pub opened for business, although its own promotional material bears a reopening date of 1958.

10. Serving the Public – Amenities and Services

The Pilot Inn was improved and refurbished in 2012

A further facility offered at this time was day fishing boat hire, whilst outside the pub was an upturned boat that served as a herring hang for the smoking of bloaters. Inside, the game of ring the bull was played. A highly popular pub pastime on the Marsh at that time, it has unfortunately all but died out now, but The Pilot is one of (probably) only two pubs[20] in the area where it can still be enjoyed. The basic equipment is in the back bar, but its use is probably best avoided when the pub is busy.

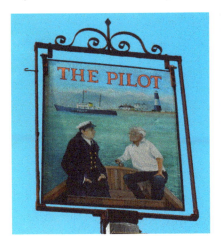

A significant benefit of the new site is that it affords its customers excellent views of shipping in the Channel, and seating and tables have been positioned to take full advantage of this. It is also on the main coast road, so able to tap into passing trade. The Pilot has built on its nautical connections over the years and taken advantage of the availability of locally caught fresh fish to develop a strong reputation for its fish-and-chip meals. The pub does, of course, owe its name to the Channel Pilot Station that operated from close to its former and present sites. For years, this link was reflected in its sign. This is an excellent representation of one of the pilots being taken out by tender (fishing boat) to the pilot cutter. It also accurately depicts the fourth (1904) lighthouse in its original – operational – black and white colours. Although no longer hanging outside the pub, the sign has been preserved and is now displayed inside. It is sited in the corridor by the toilets, but well worth seeking out. Also of interest is the large-screen television, which shows live shipping movement in the Channel, via a Coastguard feed.

---

20. The other known pub is the Shepherd & Crook at Burmarsh.

Ales by the Rails

Arguably more akin to a garden shed than a traditional pub, Ales on the Rails can best be described (just like the Snack Shack) as being typically "of Dungeness". The striking hand-painted signs of black and red design are by Dungeness artist Paddy Hamilton.

Ales by the Rails was initially a joint venture between brewer Matt Calais of the Romney Brewery and the RH&DR (in the restaurant garden of which it stands). Established in June 2017, at a time when microbreweries were starting to have a significant impact on the market, the idea was partly borne out of lack of space at the brewery for its own tap room. It has been widely described as "the smallest pub in Kent", a claim which is unlikely to be disputed. It dispenses real ale from two handpumps, as well as a selection of other drinks, including ciders and gin. Its opening was attending by local dignitaries who included the mayor of New Romney and the Hythe & Folkestone MP, all of whom travelled from New Romney on the (Romney Ales sponsored) RH&DR bar car. Matt Calais summed things up perfectly:

> Romney Marsh is totally unique. We wanted our brewery tap-room to celebrate this special landscape. A brewery beer garden right on the shingle beach, next to the railway tracks where the engines pull in, really seemed to encapsulate the inimitable spirit of Romney Marsh.

Ales by the Rails has never maintained set hours, but generally opens at weekends during high season railway service operation. At the end of the 2018 season, Matt Calais donated the building to the light railway, which continues to operate it on the same basis.

Cafes, stores and shops

Tearooms/restaurants

Now that Dungeness receives up to a million visitors a year, it is understandable that there are a number of outlets to satisfy the demand for refreshment. Yet some basic services have been provided to both visitors and residents since the 1920s, when Dungeness was far from anything approaching a tourist attraction.

Unfortunately, even less has been recorded of many of these enterprises than of other areas of Dungeness life. Most concerns appear to have been transitory, and few were listed in

10. Serving the Public – Amenities and Services

directories of the time. A number of postcards and family photographs have survived, but, as most of those predate living memory, we are dependent on second-hand accounts; and individuals appear to have been told – or recall – differing accounts by older relatives. Where there are significant differences, I have tried to take a pragmatic approach; but caveats must be applied to much of what appears in this section. As detailed in Chapter 3, The Snack Shack has also recently been established to provide fresh fish meals.

Most accounts suggest that a tea rooms situated near the RH&DR station – on the right-hand side of the top photograph below (which dates from the early 1930s) – was the first such facility at Dungeness. This may have been the case, if it was the same business as operated by the Lusted family. For a less-often published photograph (the lower one below) shows The Rest tea rooms operating in the early–mid 1920s. Recollections passed down through the generations suggest that the Lusted enterprise was quite entrepreneurial, tapping into the increasing number of beach fishermen, who would buy ice creams in the summer and hot drinks most of the year. Unfortunately, these recollections do not include its exact location. Although not conclusive, the two photographs do suggest that this could be the same building.

The Lusteds seemingly built up quite a regular trade, and were looking forward to the extension of the RH&DR, which would bring in a new market. Unfortunately for them, however, the railway decided to open its own facility. Nevertheless, it seems that the Lusteds may instead have diversified (see below).

The tea rooms near the RH&DR station (o the right of the picture above) and (left) the Lusted family tearooms, clearly showing the railway carriage family accommodation

The RH&DR catering facilities have themselves undergone many incarnations over the years. When the Dungeness station opened, there was initially a large café with living accommodation above. For much of its time, this café opened only when the railway was operating, and for a number of years the service was outsourced (with Eileen Bates being one of its principal franchisees).

The End of the Line Restaurant, soon after its opening in 2017

The End of the Line Restaurant offers excellent views across the 'Ness, as well as providing much needed shelter in bad weather

10. Serving the Public – Amenities and Services

After various modifications and refurbishments, an extensive rebuild was commenced in 2016, but problems were experienced when the contractor went into liquidation. Nevertheless, the new End of the Line Restaurant did finally open in July 2017, with the formal ceremony undertaken by musician Roger Daltrey the following month. In a nod to the tradition of its fish-and-chip suppers – and also the quirkiness of Dungeness culture – this involved the removal of old newspapers, rather than the usual pulling back of a curtain, from the commemorative plaque. The restaurant now opens all year round, providing a service to the many visitors to the area, rather than just patrons of the railway.

Post Office services

Most communities, no matter how small, had a post office from the late 19th century, or even earlier. These were commonly shops or even family homes, with the owner acting as an agent. Certainly, the Watering House was – predictably – acting as an agent at around the turn of the twentieth century, and the Bates family were still operating a post office from Spion Kop in the 1930s – which was accordingly the first property to have a telephone installed. When a telegram was received, Mrs Bates would open her front door and blow a whistle – a signal for her neighbour, Mrs Tart, to come running. Mrs Tart would then deliver the telegram to recipients up to two miles away.[21]

The date of the demise of Spion Kop's post office is unknown, but by the 1940s, its services were being discharged from a nearby bungalow, Anchorage. The telephone and post boxes still in place outside Anchorage today confirm this usage.

It seems that Anchorage provided the service up until 1947, when the post office in Battery Road opened. Now long-closed, the Battery Road building has also reverted to residential use, but remains identifiable – as the photographs demonstrate.

Shops and studios

In addition to fish and fishing products (as described in Chapter 3), a number of residents have sold goods of various descriptions from their homes, although not all have been formally registered as traders.

The common consensus is that there was a shop in the small row of properties between the Britannia Inn and the RH&DR spur, and another closer to the Sanctuary. The most well known was the Central Stores, as it features in a number of postcards of the mid-late 1930s. It was destroyed by a bomb during WWII, although fortunately nobody was inside at the time. The photographic evidence suggests that this may well have been the former tea rooms situated near the RH&DR station – and the fact that it also offered teas lends support to this theory. Whether it would have been run by the Lusteds at this time is also unknown; another family believed to have traded in the village was the Eppseys.

---

21. As this predated the first road into Dungeness, the use of backstays was routinely required.

Anchorage, one of the former post offices at Dungeness

The Coast Stores & Post Office in its heyday (top). Despite the addition of a pitched roof, the building is still recognisable (bottom) – and bears the name The Old Post Office

10. Serving the Public – Amenities and Services

Jane Adams also ran what was euphemistically referred to as a general store from her home in the shadow of the fourth lighthouse. This small shop stocked fruit and vegetables, groceries and confectionery, as well as being licensed to sell tobacco products. It seems to have operated from around 1915 into the 1930s but, given that this predates the building of the estate road, one wonders just how fresh the fruit and vegetables may have been!

Inevitably, Spion Kop operated a small shop (concurrently with the Post Office) from between the wars until the late 1940s. There was also, at one time, a sweet shop operated from one of the railway carriage cottages (in the vicinity of The Sanctuary and possibly run by

The Central Stores and Tearooms, c. 1937 (above) and Jane Adams's store (left), with her son, Bob, posing outside

Stan Lake) whilst, on a larger scale, Ken and Sylvia Oiller ran what was known as a fisherman's co-operative from their Beach Cottage home. This specialised in smocks, sou'westers, sea boots and other protective equipment for those going to sea, but additionally sold sweets, drinks and other provisions.

The completion of the coast road and the corresponding influx of passing traffic also provided scope for retail services along the section known as Battery Road. The first enterprise (pre-dating even M&M Richardson) was a general store and café run by a Mr Bryant, which opened in 1937. This was known at various times as both the Dungeness Shop and Lydd Coast Stores. Bryant was bought out by a Mr Pleasants in the late 1940s,[22] and it seems that his interest was in taking over the post office function from Anchorage (as described above). From then it traded as the Coast Stores & Post Office although, after four or five years, Pleasants dispensed with the café side of the enterprise.

The fact that Dungeness has become of such interest to both tourists and artists means that many studios have sprung up over the years. These are too numerous to mention in entirety, and most have been transitory. The major exception is that operated for over 20 years by photographer Chris Shore and artist Helen Taylor, from their home, Caithness – one of the original railway carriage buildings.[23]

Caithness, the studio of Chris Shore and Helen Taylor, which hosts (outside) an ever-increasing artwork comprising items found washed up on the beach

---

22. Once again, there is a mis-match within local records. Pleasants is shown in most sources as acquiring the business in 1949, but this does not fully accord with the *Anchorage* post office closing in 1947.
23. Comprising two carriages and a horse wagon (providing linkage).

11

Ownership, Tourism and Management

History of land ownership (to 2015)

Way back in the 17th century, most of the 'Ness was owned by Richard Tufton, who later became Earl of Thanet. On his death, the estate passed to the Coke family, via his daughter Margaret – who was married to Thomas Coke of Holkham, Norfolk (as described previously). Since then, the rather unusual history of land ownership at Dungeness has resulted in some more lasting complications.

It seems, from various actions, that the main interest of the Tufton family was in protecting their income from the lighthouse (via light dues) and there is no reason to believe that the Cokes saw things much differently. The land was of little obvious commercial value and the few who wanted to settle here (mainly fishermen) usually rented a smallholding for a nominal sum. Others seemingly just fenced off a piece of land and erected a shack with no thought of going through official channels. In time, by default they would get to own the land on which their dwellings were situated. Such practices were not confined to Dungeness, although parts of this stretch of coast have been described as being administered "like the wild west".

In the 1870s, when permission was granted for the building of a railway line from Ashford, the South Eastern Railway purchased most of the land previously owned by the

Coke family. At this time, it still had only limited value over and above that as a track bed and those fishermen who had built dwellings on the northern part of the estate were left in peace. It was only when the Southern Railway encouraged staff to buy redundant carriages and stand them on land they leased from the railway for a peppercorn rent that problems started to stack up for the future. This was still years before the 1947 Planning Act laid down significant restrictions on development.

Even well into the 20th century, various actions and transactions (both formal and informal in nature) meant that there was considerable debate over the ownership of some pockets of land. This was brought into focus by a court action in 1934. The plaintiff was Robert Young Tart, a 67-year-old fisherman, who told the court that he had been fishing at Dungeness since 1877 and had bought his cottage in 1891 from a Mrs Holbrook. The previous tenant had been Fred Oiller and, before him, Charles Oiller – so the fishing credentials of the property were indisputable. Tart had taken the matter to court because the defendant had laid a water pipe between his property and the shingle – which he had considered to be his own land. There was further the complication of ownership rights over "new" land (shingle) thrown up by the action of longshore drift. The plaintiff was seeking only nominal damages (of one shilling), but the outcome of the case is not, unfortunately, recorded. It is highly interesting to note, however, that the defendant was a Mr Cyril (CE) Andrews. Andrews was the somewhat controversial property developer highly influential in the development of Greatstone, Lydd-on-Sea and parts of Littlestone. This episode confirms that he also tried (unsuccessfully) to move into the Dungeness estate.

The railway network went through a further reorganisation, with assets becoming owned by British Rail, who later sold off this land holding to Gordon (GT) Paine. This is yet another area where recorded events seem to differ from what has been passed down through the generations. The popular and frequently recounted version of events is that Paine purchased the

11. Oversight – Ownership, Management and Tourism

land in 1964 and that, when he died in 1985, it was transferred into a family trust. Conveyance documents, however, show that Paine paid £6,530 for the estate, and a number of freehold properties, on 6 December 1950. It was the family trust that was created in 1964 and continued after Gordon's death, in 1982 – not 1985.

For some residents, Paine's purchase of the estate was a pivotal event. There were questions as to whether he did actually have title to all of the land that he presided over, although this was not an uncommon situation with coastal plots. Even today, opinions are split as to his motives. Paine (listed in the accompanying legal documents as a farmer and grazier) was clearly part of a wealthy family and he saw himself as something of a philanthropist. Certain actions support this: the fact that he served as secretary of the local RNLI branch for over 50 years, helped to found the Lydd branch of St John's Ambulance, and served as a JP (as well as many other examples of public service) is much to his credit; and some are adamant that he was a good and well-respected landlord.

Those who would suggest otherwise point to his policy of operating very short-term leases and to some quite arbitrary decision-making. He would allow tenants to buy freeholds if (in his opinion) they lived there full time, and sometimes only if they could prove that they owned a properly registered boat. Paine had a zero-tolerance approach to anyone who modified their property without his prior permission; one couple who had added an unauthorised extension was apparently given the ultimatum: sell your property to Paine or he would demolish it. What did prove to be really contentious, however, was his refusal to allow anyone to own more than one property on the estate. This hit certain families – notably the Bates – hard. They were required to sell additional properties to Paine, and many drew the conclusion that he was trying to exploit the situation for financial gain.[1]

---

1. Apologists suggest that this action was probably driven by his solicitor, but it is difficult to draw any other inference.

During the majority of the Paine tenure, there were few outward signs of major long-term change on the estate. Whilst the building of the power station and subsequent transportation of gravel resulted in much greater volumes of traffic, the power station paid for the upkeep of a section of the approach road, and the extraction companies for the rest – so there was no cost to be borne by individuals or families. The only significant change in ownership was the sale of a strip of land on the west of the estate (the Trapping Area and Long Pits) to Hall Aggregates (South East) Ltd in 1986.[2] In terms of management, the family trust did later agree to offer those tenants with three-month arrangements the option of 99-year leases (although this would take until 1999 to become operative[3]).

When the estate was put on the market in 2015, the environment in which the Trust operated had changed quite significantly in the 65 years since the Paine family had first become involved – and there was no guarantee that a new owner would be philanthropic. Dungeness had by now become a highly unlikely tourist attraction and the estate road had suffered significantly as a result, being pot-holed to the extent that it was highly dangerous. Major investment was needed, but the aggregates companies were no longer involved, so who was going to pay? And, increasingly, properties were undergoing major modernisation and changing hands for huge sums, precluding future generations of 'Nessers from aspiring to ever own their own home here; questions were asked as to whether a new owner would address – or even care about – these issues.

Land adjoining the Dungeness estate has a number of different owners. In addition to those that are more obvious – the RSPB, EDF Energy and Trinity House – other pockets are owned and administered by Lydd Town Council and the ARC aggregates company. Just to the north of Dungeness, the Folkestone & District Water Co. also have a holding. The RH&DR does not own any land, but has the right to run its tracks across the shingle in perpetuity.

Growing impact of tourism

The reasons for Dungeness having become so popular and attractive to both visitors and home owners are many and complex. Although it would be wrong to single out just one, the name Derek Jarman must loom large in any attempt at an explanation.

Jarman, who was born in 1942, was a celebrated film director, stage designer and artist, who later turned to writing and indulging his passion for gardening. A fierce advocate of gay rights, he acquired Prospect Cottage with his partner, Keith Collins, just after being diagnosed as being HIV positive in 1987. Because of the need to return to London on a regular basis to honour work commitments, he made Dungeness his bolt-hole, and poured his energies into

---

2. Later being taken over by Cemex UK.
3. A move that prompted Shepway Council to anticipate pressure for new development, uncontrolled extensions to existing dwellings and the enclosure of plots.

11. Oversight – Ownership, Management and Tourism

Prospect Cottage *was built around 1910, and is pictured (left) in 1924, when still in the hands of the Richardson family. The picture on the right shows it post "Jarmanisation" (2017)*

developing the cottage garden. Following his death in 1994, and the publication of a number of books that featured Prospect Cottage,[4] the garden has become a place of pilgrimage. Visitors come from all over the world (including many from Japan) to photograph the garden, the cottage and the inscription from John Donne's poem *The Sun Rising* on the side wall of the property.

Many who do not know the place well might take the view that Jarman's open homosexuality and love of the arts would not have endeared him to the people of Dungeness. There were certainly some issues, but these were largely to do with his habit of taking for his garden anything off the beach that took his fancy, as well as the increased number of people that his presence drew to the village. For Jarman's quirkiness and his willingness to play an active part in the community meant that many established 'Nessers were quick to embrace him as one of their own. The same also applied to Collins, who became a crew member on one of the fishing boats. The house was still owned by Collins, who maintained it in the style of Jarman right up until his own death in 2018. It remains in private ownership and is not open to the public, but neither is it off-limits to visitors. Unfortunately, many members of the public seemingly have no respect for personal space or privacy and regard it as their right to roam freely around the garden and peer in through the windows.

Many other factors have also contributed to the increased popularity of Dungeness. Not least is the need of the media to fill increasing volumes of space. The vast expanse of shingle, the preservation of the fishing beach, recent architectural innovation and the many contrasts in a place so relatively close to London, all combine to ensure that it is of ongoing interest to journalists. Whenever there is a slow summer's news day, there is a good chance of a major newspaper sending a reporter down to Kent to write about its qualities, eulogize over Prospect Cottage and perpetuate the falsehood that Dungeness is Britain's only desert.

---

4. See Appendix B.

As well as through the written page, the village has received generous exposure via film and television. Two early films probably did not do a lot for tourism at the time, but stand out for depicting how the landscape once looked; they are recommended viewing for anyone with a love of Dungeness or the wider Romney Marsh. The first of these – *The Loves of Joanna Godden* (1947) – stars a young Googie Withers, who is shown running on the beach near to where the power station now stands. The other – a 1951 production starring Maxwell Reed in the title role of *The Dark Man* – shows some fascinating shots of the beach, the 1904 lighthouse and the standard gauge railway line (with sidings branching off), as well as footage of a coastguard lookout and Lydd Ranges. Much later, the 1981 cult film *The Time Bandits* included a short sequence filmed on Dungeness Beach. In common with *The Dark Man*, the 1998 Rachel Weiss film *I Want You* includes scenes not only of Dungeness, but also various locations between there and Hastings. Many TV documentaries have featured the area, and even prime time entertainment shows, such as (the aforementioned) *Eastenders* and the Inspector Lynley Mysteries, have had complete episodes shot here. Some of these have undoubtedly helped to promote interest in and focus attention on Dungeness.[5]

Another big draw of Dungeness is that, currently, it remains a free resource. This applies not only to access to the estate, but also to parking. With some other nearby resorts – such as Camber – charging up to £12 to park for a day, many motorists choose to divert to Dungeness. Furthermore, as a result of the relentless media exposure, Dungeness has now attracted the level of interest that results in some coach companies offering it as a destination for day trips. Unfortunately, not all operators bother to check or observe the requirements for bringing their vehicles on to the estate.

A final point on the impact of increasing visitor numbers is the issue of policing. The regular presence of police officers does not, however, reflect a disproportionate level of lawlessness; these are members of the Nuclear Police force, patrolling the perimeters of the power stations. In the current political climate, power stations are a terrorist target and the growing

5. A comprehensive list of all such media work, including music videos recorded in the area, can be found in Appendix C.

11. Oversight – Ownership, Management and Tourism

number of visitors could facilitate or mask surveillance work or actions by activists. The police patrols reflect the requirement for all nuclear stations to have armed guards, which was introduced in June 2005.[6]

2015 sale of the estate

The status of the estate came under intense media spotlight in 2015, when the fact that it was up for sale was widely reported. There is still debate about the way in which this was sale was handled which, given the many interests and sensitivities, is unsurprising.

In advance of the sale, the trustees applied for planning permission to toll the estate road. It has been suggested that this was a cynical exercise to influence local opinion and facilitate a sale, but this criticism seems unfair. It is the case that the state of the road had become a huge issue – cars were even being driven onto the shingle in a bid to avoid the potholes and thus damaging the environment – and that major investment was required. Given that this situation had largely arisen from the influx of tourists, consideration of levying charges on them was understandable. Yet there were, of course, those (the owners of the old lighthouse, the RH&DR and other local businesses) who had justifiable concerns that such action would seriously impact their operations. Whatever the pros and cons, the trustees seemed fairly committed to going down the tolling route, demonstrated by measures (required by law) put in place to monitor the presence of wildlife species at the prospective site of a toll gate and the related infrastructure.

The 468-acre estate was placed on the open market by local agents Stutt and Parker in the August of that year. Offers in the region of £1.5m were invited from those interested in

The proposed toll site at the entrance to the estate, with habitat monitoring measures in place, in December 2014. The proposal was to create a loop in the road, with locals (exempt from the charge) passing on one side and visitors on the other

---

6. Not that this is a completely new risk. When Brendon Dowd and his IRA associates were jailed for terrorism offences at Manchester Crown Court in 1976, the press reported that plans had been found for attacks on several British power stations, including Dungeness.

conservation or those looking at the beach as an investment. This may seem to have been an absurdly low figure, but reflected a clause in the previous sale agreement (at a time when monetary values were a lot lower) that the estate could not be sold on for less than this sum. The advertising material advised that the estate generated an annual income in excess of £130,000 from the ground rents of residential leasehold properties, commercial fishing agreements and licences allowing the movement of shingle to protect the power station and surrounding coastline. The contract included the freeholds for 22 "chalet homes", but not the lighthouses, pub, railway or power stations.

Announcement of the sale allegedly took residents by surprise and there were complaints about a lack of consultation. The Residents' Association was incredulous: ". . . we have to read about the potential sale of the land under our feet in the press" was their indignant response. One of the trustees conceded that they needed to speak to residents now that news of the sale was in the public domain, saying "Most . . . know today, anyway", before adding: "now is the right time to pass it [the estate] on to someone who can breathe new life into Dungeness". He also confirmed that the growth of tourism in the past decade had added to the strain on the local infrastructure. The fact that the sale notice was timed for August – a notoriously slow news month – may or may not be coincidental. Many newspapers perpetuated their previous mis-reporting by claiming that "Britain's only desert is up for sale", but also dwelt on the concerns of some of the residents. For commercial reasons, the price subsequently achieved has not been disclosed, but the many expressions of interest would certainly have driven it up.

In November of the same year, it was announced that power station owners, French company EDF, had been the successful purchaser. Martin Pearson, station director, was quoted as saying:

> Dungeness B has been a huge part of the community for over 30 years; many of our employees live in the area and we bring business to local suppliers . . . [W]e're delighted to be the purchasers of the estate and want to reassure the community that it is our intention to be a responsible owner of the land

whilst Maurice Ede, for the trustees said

> after the decision was made to sell the estate it was important [that] the purchaser would have the ability, track record and correct intentions of maintaining an estate such as this and we are very happy to be passing that responsibility to EDF Energy.

On the face of it, then, everyone should have been happy. But perhaps EDF was always the likely purchaser and the deal could have been struck without going through the motions of a sale on the open market. Just two years before, the company had bought a large adjacent tract of land – some 120 hectares, which included the Long Pits lakes – from Cemex UK Operations. The Long Pits were designated as an emergency source of water for power station cooling purposes,[7] and this was a large part of the rationale behind the decision to purchase – at a price considered to be greatly in excess of the market value. A similar scenario presented itself on the Dungeness Estate where the shingle license was concerned; a new owner might have imposed restrictions, or charged disproportionately. Accordingly, both the deal and the timing seemed right for both parties.

Current Estate Management

There were clearly also good public relations reasons for EDF to go down this route, and it made sense on a number of other levels, too. Proposals to toll the access road were put on hold and the road itself was fully repaired. Yet the resurfacing of the road threw into sharp focus the problems of trying to satisfy all the divergent interest groups at Dungeness: there were now those saying that the potholes had previously acted as a traffic calming measure; and complaining that the improved surface led to excessive traffic speed. There were also many other challenges facing the new owners, resulting both from conflicting interests and from the constrictions applied by the special protected status afforded Dungeness. As a result, EDF have accordingly outsourced the management functions and their approach is now undoubtedly more professional and forward-focused than what has gone before. The issue of traffic management has not gone away, but is subject to a more scientific methodology. At the time of writing, tolling has not been discounted, but will be reviewed once new traffic census data has been analysed. Not that tolling is a black-and-white matter: leases of at least some of the local businesses (e.g. the RH&DR and the old lighthouse) stipulate free right of access for their customers. Measures to address the behaviour of motorists include monitoring of speeds, and the cracking down on regular offenders. The introduction of speed bumps and even chicanes has been considered, but these also pose potential further problems. Both would require additional lighting to be installed to satisfy safety legislation; this would further alter the character of an estate that currently has only three street lights.

Reprofiling of the parking area around the old lighthouse was undertaken in spring 2016. Whilst the introduction of a parking charge might arguably help reduce the growing strain on the infrastructure, this would require enforcement; and a serious and negative down side would be that individuals might try to avoid payment by parking on the verges, at yet more cost to the environmental balance. A measure that *has* been introduced to mitigate the impact

---

7. This is a back-up arrangement, to mitigate the risk of a tidal surge knocking out the primary pumps.

The Dungeness boardwalk (2015)

of tourism is the building of the boardwalk to the sea, between the two lighthouses. Predating EDF involvement, this leads to the shore, and was constructed to both facilitate access and protect the shingle habitat. The route does not follow a public right of way, but helps to ensure that human activity is concentrated in one small area rather than across the whole beach. It was funded from a number of different sources, reflecting some of the many groups that have an interest here.[8]

The nature of the private estate also changes the dynamic where members of the public are concerned. Many dog walkers use the site, without necessarily feeling that they are under the same constraints as if on public land. The number of visitors has inevitably resulted in an increase in litter, although the majority of this remains fishing debris. The solution to this problem has been typically innovative: the Dungeness Angling Association raises a levy on its members, which is used to fund a part-time litter warden on the estate. More recent problems have been thrown up by the increased ownership of drones; their use on the estate is now banned, as are 4×4 vehicles from entering the beach. Up to 200 fashion shoots a year are staged on the 'Ness and, now, prior permission is required to undertake such activity. This regulation is again necessary to limit damage to the estate, but not all observe the requirement and it is another area that requires policing. One of the consequences of all this regulation is the increasing number of warning and information signs now appearing on the estate. The Paine family trust had been reluctant to erect signage, but the current climate makes it a necessity. As a result of the various competing pressures, it has also been deemed necessary to develop a code of conduct, which has been published on line.

---

8. The Heritage Lottery Fund, English Nature (through DEFRA's Aggregates Levy Sustainabilities fund), the Environment Agency, SE England Development Agency (SEEDA), and Community Action in South Kent (CASK).

11. Oversight – Ownership, Management and Tourism

Two of the numerous signs that are now to be found on the Dungeness estate

In increasingly litigious times, another consideration, alongside the need to preserve the environment, is the safety of those who use the estate. There is a dichotomy between maintaining a working and historic fishing beach and ensuring public safety; some of the decaying buildings have become attractive to children and, because they are inherently dangerous, require regular monitoring.

Another area that was not fully addressed by the family trust was the state of the beach. There is again a fine line between industrial history and decay on the one hand and littering on the other. For years, metal storage containers have been utilised by fishermen, but many have remained in place long after becoming redundant. This effectively constitutes dumping, prompting one well-known TV presenter to question how a part of a National Nature Reserve could so closely resemble a teenager's bedroom! To their credit, EDF have grasped the nettle and at the time of writing are preparing a clearance programme for such containers.

Iconic, but falling apart – one of the photogenic fishing shacks that now poses a safety risk

The fishing beach in 2018, showing some of the many no-longer used fishing containers

Development and planning

It is unfortunate that the lack of demarcation of boundaries that so characterises Dungeness is interpreted by so many as an invitation to invade the privacy of homeowners, as earlier described in relation to Prospect Cottage. Although some residents choose not to have fences, in most cases planning restrictions preclude them. Those that already had fences in place in the mid-1980s (when visitors were fewer and privacy was respected) were allowed to keep them, but regulations designed to maintain environmental sight lines have precluded the installation of any new boundary structures.

This does serve to demonstrate that environmental legislation is a relatively recent constraint, but more general building controls have, for much longer, applied to the estate. Nevertheless, back in the early 20th century, there was very little developmental regulation at Dungeness. The fishermen were more or less allowed to get on with things as they saw fit at the northern end, whilst, from the 1920s, the railway companies dictated what happened in the south of the village. The 1986 Conservation Plan described Dungeness as a "Frozen Mobile Settlement", with reference to the unplanned and uncontrolled nature of much of the building, as well as the "accidental architecture" that had proliferated prior to the Town & Country Planning Act of 1947. There would anyway have been few families or homeowners in a position to either want or be able to afford any substantial development. Nor would there have been many other "outsiders" looking to move into the village up until this time. When the estate became within the control of the Paine family, the policy of not adding to the existing housing stock was maintained. There was still no great appetite for development, although, when later under the administration of trustees, a few residents successfully applied to rebuild their homes to more lavish specifications.

There remained concerns, from those not fully conversant with planning laws, that a new owner might seek to radically develop the estate. But, as Maurice Ede subsequently said of the 2015 sale (specifically in relation to development):

11. Oversight – Ownership, Management and Tourism

No planning or development restrictions were in place in the 1920s when these carriages first appeared on the beach (Chris Shore collection)

> It shouldn't affect the residents very much at all . . . [On] top of that there are planning restrictions placed by the local authority which are very stringent. So there's no way [new owners] can come in and build houses all over it.

It may be incongruous, therefore, that one of the numerous factors that has brought Dungeness into the mainstream media spotlight is the many awards its buildings have recently achieved for innovative design. Admittedly, these are for single-storey property rebuilds on the same sites, often with the same footprint; and all have received the necessary planning permissions.

Aside from the usual gripes about personal and vested interest, the actions of the planning authorities have genuinely puzzled many residents. It is just possible, though, to sympathise with the authorities, because it is so difficult to know exactly how to treat Dungeness. For, as a resident has been quoted as saying: "Dungeness is both unintentional and deliberate at the same time; how can you decide whether something is *in keeping*?". Many would argue that the lasting appeal of Dungeness lies in its diversity; and that, with its industrial fishing beach, two lighthouses, power stations, converted wartime buildings, railway carriages, fishing huts and state-of-the-art designs, it is very difficult to reject something on the grounds of incompatibility or "being different".

Where the planners have tried to find compromise, owners and architects have conspired to exploit the nonsense of planning regulations. Innovation has often related as much to interpretation of planning laws as to design. For example, where the former railway-carriage homes are concerned, the main planning criterion appears to be a need to preserve or maintain the integrity of the original structure. This has resulted in (as with El Ray and Channel View) a completely new design constructed around the original. The outcomes can be quite impressive

The interior of Stonihoe (between the two lighthouses) shows just how stunning the old railway carriage constructions can still be, given the right care and attention (photo courtesy Stephanie Ingham/Holiday Cottages)

when viewed internally, but for much of the time the original remains invisible from the outside. It is also a moot point whether the planning authorities intend to follow up to ensure that their requirements continue to be met.

The debate has recently been refocused by the 2018/19 development of the Marconi/Decca building. Whilst it was a structure that unquestionably fell within the "iconic" category, there can be little doubt that it had deteriorated to such an extent that economic repair was out of the question. A full restoration would also have been pointless: it could have served no purpose. Yet a planning application that was submitted with a view to demolition and replacement with a modest bungalow was initially turned down, despite two years of detailed negotiations involving Natural England and residents – because consensus could not be achieved. More generally, opinions have been expressed that the views of incomers, who do not even live full-time on the 'Ness, carry more weight than those of families who have lived here for

The building that replaced the Decca research station under construction, in April 2018

generations. There is probably some truth in this, but rather because second home owners tend to be more *au fait* with planning regulations – and how to get around them.

To understand the planning arguments and concerns better, it is worth while exploring some of the rebuilt properties that have received so much attention and (often) planning awards.

El Ray

El Ray is one of the four properties situated to the east of the power station and south of the 1904 lighthouse. Designed by Simon Conder Associates, the rebuild – which is bell-shaped – was completed in 2008. It has won both Kent Design and RIBA (Royal Institute of British Architects) awards for buildings costing under £1m.

The former building comprised the original 19th railway carriage, which had been extended at each end. It was in very poor condition and too small for the growing family that inhabited it. After restoration, the carriage was retained in the centre (forming part of the kitchen) and the accommodation increased by 50 percent by the simple expedient of building around it. A rooftop wind turbine is now used to provide additional energy for underfloor heating.

Vista

On the beach side of the road, close to the new lighthouse, is the distinctive timber and plywood building encased in a rubber-type cladding, which goes by the name of Vista. It was completed in 2003 as a weekend retreat for a London family – a growing and not unfamiliar scenario. It stands on the site of one of the most southerly of the 1920s/1930s fisherman's cottages, which was another that had fallen into disrepair. The cladding acts as in the same way as a wet suit, providing very good insulation, and allows the whole building to be effectively heated by a small stove.

Also designed (as El Ray) by architect Simon Conder, it was awarded the Stephen Lawrence Prize[9] for the best building on a budget of £350,000. The judges praised the house

---

9. Part of the Royal Institute of British Architects (RIBA) award scheme, sponsored by the Marco Goldschmied Foundation and named after the London teenager (who had aspirations to be an architect) murdered in a senseless racist attack.

The rubber-clad Vista, 2017

for having a "carefully controlled witticism"; although to any normal person, this says far more about the pretentiousness of the architectural community than anything meaningful about the bungalow. The black colour scheme is typical of local fishing settlements (many Hastings and Rye, as well as Dungeness, fishermen's buildings display similar characteristics) and one of the more unusual aspects is a bathroom window that commands views of the sea – but presumably offers precious little privacy – for anyone lying in the bath.

Pobble House

In July 2013, Peace Haven, a dilapidated bungalow on the landward side of the road (close to the RH&DR's Britannia Points) was demolished, in accordance with planning permission granted for a rebuild. Designed by Guy Holloway Architects and completed in 2014, the rebuilt property was named the Pobble House, recalling the old Kentish word for pebble. It was constructed with materials purportedly selected to weather "sympathetically", so as to blend in better with the natural landscape. It was also built slightly off the ground, on concrete columns, to avoid undue damage to the shingle beach.

In 2015, the Pobble House won a RIBA regional award (the awards' judges – presumably drawing inspiration from the nonsense spouted by their colleagues in relation to El Ray – commenting on the "highly personal and contextual design for an exclusive holiday retreat that will respond to the history of its unique environment").

It was also shortlisted for the Sunday Times British Homes Award. Despite the hyperbole, there are many (both locals and visitors) who feel that this building does address the conflict between tradition and the need to modernise far better than most of its contemporaries.

11. Oversight – Ownership, Management and Tourism

The Shingle House, 2017

The Shingle House

Originally another fisherman's cottage (going by the name of Pearl Cottage), The Shingle House is also close to the RH&DR line, a little to the north of Prospect Cottage. Its metamorphosis caused more concern amongst residents than many of the other rebuilds, because of the history of the place: it had formerly housed a prominent smokery, and all traces of this were obliterated in the process.[10]

Surprisingly, this building was designed by a Scottish practice, the Northern Office for Research and Design (NORD). The highly distinctive black building has two large, full-length windows and a sheltered inner courtyard. It has impressive views, both over the sea and across the 'Ness to the power stations and Lydd.

Channel View

Channel View also started out life in Dungeness as a Victorian railway carriage, which was later extended with the addition of a lean-to.

Because planning conditions once more required the original structure to be retained, the carriage was removed for repair, after the extension had been demolished. Channel View, like many of its neighbours, was originally set on railway sleepers, so a new concrete base was laid, on to which the

---

10. See Chapter 2.

carriage was subsequently repositioned. This now forms an intriguing internal centrepiece to the new property.

Experimental Station

The Trinity House Experimental Station was a pioneering establishment, so it is probably fitting that its reincarnation has been widely praised for innovative design. The brainchild of architect Brian Johnson, co-founder of the Johnson Naylor architect and design practice, the conversion was not without its share of problems.

The original buildings contained asbestos and other contaminants and some – such as the former generator house – had (and continue to have) extremely thick walls, as they were built to withstand explosions. Furthermore, the floors in some rooms had to be raised to conform with building regulations, which require any sleeping areas to be a minimum height above sea level.

Up to 20 different designs and combinations were considered before planning permission for development was finally granted. The centrepiece is now the former fog-signal building (which once housed the compressors) and which has become a pavilion with windows affording 360-degree views. Completed in 2013, it has won two regional RIBA awards.

The old fog signal building, now let out as holiday accommodation (2017)

Into the future

The above conversions have brought into sharp focus the issues for and against modernisation. There is a view that Dungeness is becoming a showcase for contemporary architecture, and this does cause consternation to those locals who remain. Certainly, where these properties are concerned, there is little chance of the younger generation being able to afford to buy, and if these continue to become just weekend retreats or holiday lets, the soul of the village will be lost. Many argue that the point of no return has already been passed, with less than half the properties now being occupied full-time. Some homes are being sold for inflated prices, without consideration of their condition; it is the site that is in demand, with purchasers often intent on rebuilding from the outset.

Against this background, some locals are happy to sell, knowing that the excess of demand over supply either enables them to buy much larger homes nearby or provides them with a hefty lump sum for investment or retirement. The old railway carriages that remain are mostly Victorian and well beyond their shelf-life, so responsible modernisation is surely preferable to dwellings just being allowed to rot *in situ*. There has been a perceptible change in the attitudes of some residents in recent years, although this may rather reflect that there are fewer indigenous 'Nessers left to offer their thoughts. More practically, there is no longer a thriving fishing community to protect, and the carriage owners do not have the same rich heritage to consider as their predecessors. Another contentious issue is that byelaws and lease conditions – imposed in a bid to preserve both the environment and community – have not always been enforced in recent times. These include regulations that still theoretically preclude anyone owning more than one property on the estate.

Regardless of the debate surrounding progress and the need to balance this with tradition, something to which most take exception is the regular name changes of some of these properties. This is not something that just applies to rebuilds, such as Pobble House and The Shingle House. Retreat, for example, (the one building located within the turning loop of the RH&DR) recently became Quatre Vents; Windwhistle has become Providence via a few other changes; Haford is now Yale; and Sea Patch has become Triumph. In addition to the confusion that this must cause postal and other delivery personnel (none of the properties are numbered), this undermines tradition and provides no obvious benefit.

It cannot be denied that the fishing community that *was* Dungeness for the bulk of the 20th century has largely disappeared. The lifeboat is no longer crewed by Oillers, Tarts and Richardsons and the once-popular community events such as the Christmas minstrel procession and the May Day Parade and fun day are no more. This may reflect wider societal trends, but – for many – it is a great sadness. And, whilst the plans for a 19th/20th century port

Nanny Goat Island

never came to fruition, larger scale, external threats to the community continue to surface from time to time. Periodically, the ferry terminal proposal has been revived, with greater or lesser degrees of credibility. Most notable was a scheme put forward in April 1971 at the height of the oil boom, which resulted in front-page headlines in all the local newspapers. Such stories are often "planted" by those with a political or economic axe to grind, but this had some substance to it, with the established consulting engineers G Maunsell & Partners commissioned to produce a preliminary appraisal.[11] This considered the creation of a major deep-water port capable of handling giant oil tankers of up to 500,000 tons. Once discharged, the oil would have been piped to refineries across the Channel, as well as to others in the Medway and Thames. In order to realise this plan, nearly 700 acres of land would have had to have been reclaimed from the sea and the cost of phase 1 alone was estimated to be in excess of £100m. The same factors that had made Dungeness attractive to earlier entrepreneurs still applied and the success of the power station had opened the eyes to those who doubted that such a remote location could accommodate a major infrastructure project. Nevertheless, Folkestone and Hythe MP Albert Costain, whilst acknowledging that the concept was attractive, spoke for many in opining that it was "pie in the sky". Although a port development could still happen in the future, it must be considered most unlikely. A greater and more tangible risk to the Dungeness landscape is the development of Lydd Airport. Plans for transforming Lydd into a third London airport first emerged in 1968 and have regularly resurfaced. There can be no doubt that, should a major expansion of Lydd Airport ever be sanctioned, it really would spell the end of Dungeness as we know it.

---

11. It has never been definitively established just who funded this work.

12

A Final Mystery

There are many unanswered questions surrounding Dungeness, some of which stretch back centuries. Yet one of the most baffling first raised its head only in the 1990s. At this time, a stone figure appeared on the beach at Denge Marsh (about 50 yards north of the Myrtle Cottage memorial). It is too good a sculpture to have been produced as a prank and, although there has been constant speculation as to its origin, nobody has yet identified its creator or come forward with a satisfactory explanation for its presence.

Despite some signs of weathering, the Stone Man of Dungeness remains as a dramatic and somewhat disturbing piece of art. Some have surmised that he is a memorial to those who died in the two world wars; others that he is a tribute to those who suffered in the Chernobyl nuclear disaster; and still others that he more generally represents man's struggle with nature. Whilst we may never know, he seems to perfectly capture the mystery and romance of this astonishing place.

Appendix A

Detailed Timeline

(Note: in some cases, dates are only approximate)

Pre-19th century

1521: First record of a hermit living at St Mary's Chapel (at 'The Nesse, Lydd').

1526: Fellowship of the Cinque Port Pilots established to protect pilots in the Channel and resist foreign competition.

1615: First (coal-fired) Dungeness lighthouse.

1633: Spanish vessel *Alfresia* wrecked, and part of its hull used to augment the first Pilot Inn.

1635: Second (coal-fired) lighthouse.

1640: Matthew Poker's map of Romney Marsh shows a number of fishermen's cabins at Dungeness.

1652: Battle of Dungeness (part of Anglo-Dutch war).

1792: Third Dungeness lighthouse (initially oil-fired; later powered by electricity).

1793/94: Likely date of construction of No. 1 battery, in advance of other batteries and redoubt.

1795: Construction of Royal Naval Shore Signal Station (RNSSS).

1798: Work begins on construction of batteries 2, 3 and 4; and of the Dungeness Redoubt.

19th century

1802: Dungeness RNSSS de-activated.

1803: Dungeness Signal Station re-established. First unofficial lifeboat cover, provided from Rye.

1803/4: Admiralty and Trinity House agree that, in conditions of poor visibility, lookout staff may be based on top floor of lighthouse.

1810: Watch House (Watch Tower) constructed.

1812: Pilot cutters anchored off Dungeness for first time.

1813: 12,000 gallons of smuggled brandy landed at Dungeness in a single week.

1814: Dungeness Signal Station again closed.

1816: Counter-smuggling Coast Blockade Service (CBS) created, operating between Dungeness and North Foreland.

1818: Dungeness Signal Station once more resurrected, as part of ongoing battle against smuggling.

1818–1823: Batteries 3 and 4 (to west of Dungeness Point) destroyed by sea.

1820: First RNSSS staff accommodation built in redoubt.

1826: St Mary's Bay lifeboat (designated "Dungeness") station opens.

1832: British Sailor pub opens at Galloways.

1837: "Dungeness Station" (St Mary's Bay) lifeboat severely damaged, which leads to closure of station.

1840: Watering House constructed (Note: this may even date to a few years earlier).

1850: British Inn (Britannia) opens.

1852: Two major incidents off Dungeness result in renewed calls to restore local lifeboat cover.

1854: First lifeboat station opens at Dungeness.

1860: No. 1 battery remodelled and reinforced to accommodate five heavier guns.

1860s: First of the fishing cottages that we would recognise today constructed at northern end of village.

1861: Dungeness lifeboat relocated to Littlestone.

1864: Lydd Lifesaving Company formed.

1865: *The Brooks* requisitioned by Army. George Remington draws up detailed plans for railway tunnel between Dungeness and France.

1870s: Lady lifeboat launchers first involved. Much of Dungeness purchased from Coke family by South Eastern Railway.

1873: British vessel *Northfleet* sinks, with loss of 293 lives, three miles off Dungeness. Rye & Dungeness Railway & Pier Company authorised to construct a railway line from Rye to Dungeness, together with a port and pier.

1874: Dungeness lifeboat station re-instated.

1877: Dungeness School ("The School Beautiful") established.

1878: Construction of coastguard cottages at entrance to estate.

Early 1880s: First Lloyds Signal station opens.

1881: Appledore–Lydd (for passenger traffic) and Dungeness (freight) lines open.

1882: Act to extend branch line from Dungeness to New Romney passed.

1883: Dungeness rail section opened to passenger traffic. Lloyds Signal Station moves to Lloyds Cottage.

1884: New Romney branch line (Lydd–New Romney) completed. First Dungeness low light (with fog signal) constructed.

1885: Joseph Castle appointed assistant curate at Lydd, and takes up duties as "curate to the coast".

1887: First self-righting lifeboat installed at Dungeness.

1888: Dungeness Cricket Club formed.

Early 1890s: Dutch consulate engages Bates family to log and report details of Dutch shipping.

1891: Lydd Lifesaving Company moves to Dungeness. Two purpose-built pilot cutters delivered to Dungeness Pilot Station. Series of violent storms in the year sees numerous shipwrecks, and three crew members die after their lifeboat capsizes.

1892: No. 2 lifeboat installed at Dungeness.

20th century

1900s

1900–1920: Most of extant fisherme's dwellings constructed.

1902: Littlestone & District Water Company construct tower at Dungeness (Dengemarsh) to supply all of New Romney and surrounding area (but not Dungeness!).

1904: Fourth (paraffin-fuelled) Dungeness lighthouse enters service.

1905: RSPB secures statutory protection for Dungeness. New RN Signal Station constructed.

1906: Kent Education Authority takes over running of Dungeness School.

1908: The RSPB appoints two "watchers" to Dungeness, to protect nesting ground birds.

1910s

1910: Old revetments constructed, to the west of Dungeness Point.

1914: Dungeness Fort constructed.

1915: Society for Protection of Nature Reserves lists Dungeness as an area of prime importance.

1917: *HMS Ghurka* strikes mine off Dungeness, with loss of 74 lives.

1918: *HMS Zubian* sinks German mine-laying submarine (UC-50) just off Dungeness Point.

1920s

1920: Southern Railway company offers its staff and pensioners the opportunity to buy redundant rolling stock, for use as holiday homes on its land at Dungeness. Date sometimes given for construction of Admiralty siding (although this has to be open to question). Also possible date for establishment of crushing plant.

Early 1920s: Introduction of pre-treated fishing nets leads to redundancy of tanning coppers. Lusted family open first tearooms at Dungeness.

1926: Britannia pub redesigned and rebuilt.

1929: Richard Burrowes buys 50 acres of land adjoining the Lydd–Dungeness road (including Boulderwall Farm). Dungeness becomes one of the first lighthouse stations to receive new wireless fog-signal technology. Imperial Airways Handley Page W.10 ditches in sea some three miles off Dungeness, with loss of seven lives.

Late 1920s: Army lookout post constructed at Dengemarsh.

1930s

Early 1930s: Central Stores opens.

1931: RSPB buys up parcels of land at Dungeness (including Walkers Outlands area) with the help of large donation from Richard Burrowes.

1932: Second Dungeness low light designed and built.

1933: First motorised lifeboat installed at Dungeness.

1935: Coast road providing circular route through Romney, Lydd Greatstone and Dungeness completed. RSPB purchases further tracts of land at Dungeness, including the Oppen Pits.

1937: Re-aligned railway line from Dungeness to New Romney opens. Dungeness station closed to passenger traffic, and new station opens at Lydd-on-Sea ("for Dungeness").

1938: Estate road constructed as far as Beach Cottage. Lydd Lifesaving Company moves to Galloways. Handley Page RAF aircraft crashes into the sea off Dungeness; neither plane nor crew are seen again.

1940s

1940: WWII evacuation of most of the coastal area (although fishermen allowed to remain – with significant conditions imposed); buildings commandeered by army. Dungeness School closes. RSPB reserve requisitioned by army for gunnery training. Steamship *MV Roseburn* torpedoed by two German E-boats off Dungeness Point. Spies Karl Heinrich Meier and Jose Waldberg land at Dungeness, but are soon captured. Dungeness Fort modified and enhanced. Dungeness lifeboat the *Charles Cooper Henderson* takes part in evacuation of allied troops from Dunkirk.

1941: Pilot Officers Boguslaw Mierzwa and Mieczyslaw Waskiewicz die after their aircraft crash at/off Dungeness.

1942: Work begins on PLUTO project.

1944: Area upgraded from restricted area to demarcation zone. American B17 Flying Fortress bomber *Sleepytime Girl* crashes into sea off Dungeness (April). Doodlebugs targeting the UK start to arrive across the Channel. PLUTO pipelines laid from Dungeness to Ambleteuse, near Boulogne. Winston Churchill visits Dungeness to witness testing of a new flame thrower.

1945: Army takes over part of Pen Bars to extend Lydd Ranges, resulting in demolition of Myrtle Cottage.

1946: Mains water laid on to Dungeness village. Following end of WWII, RH&DR first reopens section between New Romney and Maddieson's Camp as a single line. Rest of the line to Dungeness re-opens later in year. Richardson's fish business opens in Battery Road.

1947: Hope & Anchor pub (Pen Bars) closes.

1947/8: Severe winter weather prevents fishing fleet going to sea for 10 weeks.

1950s

Early 1950s: Electricity installed to Dungeness properties. Rabbits start to overrun the 'Ness.

1950: British Rail sells Dungeness estate to GT Paine.

1951: RH&DR wind pump demolished.

1952: Railway line between Romney Junction and Dungeness formally closes, and rails removed. Most of its reserve returned to the RSPB by the War Office; new warden

Herbert Axell speaks of need to control predators and conceives idea of building a lake for nesting birds. Floodlighting installed at Dungeness lighthouse in bid to reduce risk to bird population. Dungeness Bird Observatory formed. Britannia Inn burns down.

1953: Dungeness railway section closes to goods traffic. Myxomatosis first noted at Dungeness.

1954: Lydd Airport (the first new airport in the UK post-WWII) opens.

1955: Rebuilt Britannia Inn opens on current site (over foundations of WWII officer accommodation).

1956: Richard Burrowes dies at 85, leaving his land (including Boulderwall Farm) to the RSPB. The idea of a power station at Dungeness is first mooted.

1957: Electricity Link Station at Dungeness becomes operational. Test boreholes completed for proposed power station at Dungeness. Pilot Inn relocated from entrance to Dungeness estate to current site.

1958: Formal opening of Trinity House Experimental Station at Dungeness. Public enquiry held into viability of a power station.

1959: Low light and foghorn demolished to make way for new Dungeness light. Approval granted for construction of power station.

1960s

Early 1960s: Spindle Cottage demolished to make way for power station.

1960: Work begins on Dungeness A. Demolition of remains of Battery No. 1 halted (and preservation measures put in place). Dengemarsh Coastguard lookout constructed.

1961: First HVDC (High Voltage Direct Current) Cross-Channel converter completed. Electricity laid on to Dungeness estate properties. Fifth Dungeness light enters service.

1962: Last scheduled steam service on New Romney branch line.

1963: Mail van carrying power station workers' wages hijacked on the Lydd–Dungeness road.

1964: Ownership of Dungeness estate passes to Paine family trust.

1965: Dungeness A commences generation of electricity. Contract for Dungeness B power station placed.

1966: Work begins on Dungeness B power station.

1967: Closure of New Romney branch line. Dungeness pilot station also closes.

1968: MOD (Army) observation tower at Dungeness demolished.

1969: Main Dungeness B construction company enters administration.

1970s

1970: Excavation of RSPB Burrowes Pit commences (completion will take eight years). Access road to RSPB site constructed from Dungeness Road.

1975: Patch Hide (financed by CEGB) constructed on Dungeness beach.

1978: DBO erects hide overlooking the Long Pits.

Late 1970s: Construction of concrete roads to eastern Dungeness fishing beach; and from the south end of the estate road to the power station. The Earth House demolished. New Coastguard lookout opens at Dungeness.

1980s

1982: Death of GT Paine at age of 82.

1983: Dungeness B begins generation. Fierce storm destroys Dungeness waiting shelter on RH&DR.

1984: Inverter station constructed at Sellindge, rendering Dungeness HVDC obsolete.

1985: Dungeness B second reactor comes into operation.

1986: Hall Aggregates (South East) Ltd purchases Dungeness Trapping Area and Long Pits.

1987: Seawatch Hide constructed on Dungeness beach. Later in the year, hurricane destroys both this and Patch Hide. Derek Jarman buys Prospect Cottage.

1988: Last recorded sighting of short-haired bumble bee at Dungeness.

1989: New Patch and Seawatch Hides completed and handed over to DBO. Dungeness lifeboat station extended.

End 1980s: Dungeness (Trinity House) research facility closes.

1990s

Early 1990s: RSPB re-introduce grazing sheep on their reserve.

1991: New RSPB Visitor Centre opens. Dungeness lighthouse converted to automatic operation.

1993: Remains of DBO Long Pits Hide removed.

1994: New crew room added to Dungeness lifeboat station. Death of Derek Jarman.

1997: Dungeness lookout decommissioned by Coastguard Agency.

1998: Dungeness designated a National Nature Reserve. Dungeness lookout sold to private purchaser.

21st Century

2003: Current lighthouse allocated Grade II listed status.

2006: Dungeness A ceases generation.

2009: Routine maintenance at Dungeness B identifies serious problems, which result in reactor 1 being shut down for 18 months. Dungeness placed on short list of 11 sites for a new nuclear power station.

2012: Reintroduction of short-haired bumble bee (declared extinct in 2000) to Dungeness. Defueling process at Dungeness A completed.

2013: Long Pits acquired by EDF Energy.

2014: New flood wall constructed around Dungeness power station. Dungeness becomes the first station to receive the new Shannon-class lifeboat (the *Morrell*). Snack Shack opens.

2015: Dungeness estate purchased by EDF Energy. Dungeness B granted 10-year life extension. Demolition of Dungeness A turbine hall completed.

2016: New memorial to Pilot Officers Boguslaw Mierzwa and Mieczyslaw Waskiewicz erected. 16 Albanian immigrants and two UK people-smugglers rescued in the Channel by the Dungeness lifeboat.

2017: Fisherman Joe Thomas retrieves one of the radial engines of *Sleepytime Girl* from his fishing nets. New *End of the Line* Restaurant and *Ales on the Rails* micropub open at RH&DR station. Long Pits awarded the Wildlife Trusts Biodiversity Benchmark.

2018: Dungeness lifeboat rescues nine Albanian immigrants in the Channel. Decca Research Station building demolished.

Appendix B

Bibliography

Derek Jarman's Cottage – estate of Derek Jarman (Thames & Hudson Ltd, 1995, 2015)

Dungeness Lighthouses – Edward Carpenter (Margaret F Bird & Associates, 1996, 1998, 2000)

Dungeness: a unique place – ed. Ged Robinson (Sutton House [Ilford] 1998)

Flogging Joey's Warriors – John Douch (Crabwell Publications, 1985)

Front Line County: Kent at War, 1939–45 – Andrew Rootes (Robert Hale Ltd, 1980)

Front Line Kent – Michael Foley (The History Press, 2006)

Kent & Sussex 1940 – Stuart Hylton (Pen & Sword Military Books, 2004)

Military Signals from the South Coast: from Fire Beacons to the Railway Telegraph – John Goodwin (Middleton Press, 2000)

Modern Nature – Derek Jarman (Century, 1991; also Vintage Publishing, 2018)

Much Drinking in the Marsh – Keith Swallow (Edgerton Publishing Services, 2017)

Old Romney Marsh in Camera – Edward Carpenter (Birlings, 1984)

Romney Marsh – Fay Godwin & Richard Ingram (Wildwood House Ltd, 1980)

Romney Marsh – Walter JC Murray (Hale, 1953, 1972 and 1975)

Romney Marsh (Britain in Old Photographs) – Edward Carpenter (Alan Sutton Publishing, 1994)

Romney Marsh (Britain in Old Photographs; a second selection) – Edward Carpenter (Sutton Publishing, 1996)

Romney Marsh at War – Edward Carpenter (Sutton Publishing, 1999)

Romney Marsh Past & Present – Dave Randle (The History Press, 2005)

Romney Marsh Yesteryears – Edward Carpenter (Margaret F Bird & Associates, 1983)

Romney Marsh: Survival on a Frontier – Jill Eddison (Tempus Publishing, 2000)

The Coast Blockade: The Royal Navy's War on Smuggling in Kent & Sussex 1817–1831 – Roy Philp (Horsham Sussex Compton Press, 1999)

The Fifth Continent – Duncan Forbes (Shearwater Press [Kent], 1984)

The Gift of the Sea – Anne Roper (Birlings [Kent] Ltd, 1984)

The Later Kentish Seaside – Felicity Stafford & Nigel Yates (Alan Sutton, 1985)

The Natural History of Romney Marsh – Dr FM Frith (Meresborough Books, 1984)

The New Romney Branch Line – Peter A Harding (self-published, 1983)

The Romney Hythe & Dymchurch Railway – RW Kidner (Oakwood Press, 1967)

The Romney Hythe & Dymchurch Railway – WJK Davies (David & Charles, 1975, 1988)

The Romney Marsh Coastline from Hythe to Dungeness – David Singleton (The History Press, 2008)

The World's Smallest Public Railway – P Ransome Wallace (Ian Allan, 1968)

Wild Flowers of Dungeness – B Gray & H Silk (Judges, 2007)

Wrecks and Rescues off the Romney Marsh Coast – Edward Carpenter (Margaret F Bird & Associates, 1985)

Booklets without full publication details

Dungeness Remembered – Ken Oiller (Printing at New Romney; date not credited)

Joseph Castle: Curate to the Coast and Chaplain to Dungeness Coastguards 1885–1889 – Edward Carpenter & Margaret Bird

Tales of an Ordinary Dungeness Man – Ken Oiller (Printing at New Romney; date not credited)

Appendix C

Dungeness in Film and Other Media

Feature films

The Loves of Joanna Godden (1947)

A significant film of its day, this was an adaption of Sheila Kaye-Smith's celebrated book of the same name. Produced by Michael Balcon and with screenplay by HE Bates, it stars Googie Withers in the title role. The film centres on Godden's attempts to run the family farm following the death of her father, and the bigotry and chauvinism she encounters along the way. There is some excellent footage of the Romney Marsh in general and of Dungeness in particular (notably the power station site pre-development).

The Dark Man (1951)

Billed as a British thriller from Rank Studios, this film stars Edward Underdown, Maxwell Reed and Natasha Parry. The bulk of the filming took place between Hastings and Dungeness, with the final scenes exclusively at Dungeness and on the Lydd Ranges. There is good footage of the 1904 lighthouse, the two railway stations and the standard gauge railway line (including the Ballast Hole sidings). The film undoubtedly features more and better coverage of the area than any other mainstream film, and provides a very good historical record.

The Time Bandits (1981)

Terry Gilliam's fantasy film which stars Sean Connery, John Cleese and Michael Palin, amongst others. One short scene is shot on Dungeness beach, but shows very little background (there is little to identify the location as being obviously Dungeness).

Bellman & True (1987)

Film written and directed by Richard Loncraine, based on the novel of the same name by Desmond Lowden and starring Bernard Hill, Derek Newark and Richard Hope. The title is a line taken from the song *Do you ken John Peel?* and "bellman" is also slang in the criminal fraternity for a security alarm expert. The plot involves a bank raid in London, after which some of the team hide out at Dungeness. Whilst most of the film is shot in London and elsewhere, some critical scenes are set on the beach at Dungeness, with the power station in the background. The property used as the robbers' hideout is Westward Ho!, which (in the script) is blown up. This incident, despite the on-site presence of a fire engine, resulted in severe fire damage to the property (this is described in Chapter 7).

The Last of England (1987)

British arthouse film starring Tilda Swinton and directed by Dungeness resident Derek Jarman. It is a poetic depiction by Jarman, reflecting his view that traditional English culture was fast disappearing in the 1980s. The film takes its name from a work by Ford Madox Ford, who lived for some of his life in nearby Winchelsea.

War Requiem (1989)

Another Jarman-directed film, this is an adaptation of Benjamin Britten's musical work of the same name. It uses Britten's 1963 recording as the soundtrack and was shot in 1988. It includes footage of Jarman's Prospect Cottage garden, which is portrayed in different scenes as both the Garden of Eden and Gethsemane.

The Garden (1990)

A further British arthouse film directed by Jarman, revisiting some familiar themes and again featuring Tilda Swinton. The 95-minute production focuses on some of the conflicts between homosexuality and Christianity, set against the Prospect Cottage and wider Dungeness landscape. The film was entered for the 17th Moscow International Film Festival.

I Want You (1998)

An English crime film starring Alessandro Nivola as a released convict who returns home to find that his ex-girlfriend (played by Rachel Weisz) has found someone else. Dungeness features regularly, alongside other coastal settlements between there and Hastings.

The Other Man (2006)

Short movie, which won the Edinburgh Film Festival Award for Best Short Film. It stars Anna Maxwell Martin, Neal Barry and six-year-old local girl Tilly O'Neil, and includes scenes shot at Dungeness.

Una (2016)

Anglo–North American drama based upon David Harrower's play *Blackbird*. Starring Rooney Mara in the title role, it depicts a young woman attempting to reclaim her past. A number of scenes were shot at both Dungeness and Lydd-on-Sea.

Appendix C. The Area in Film and Other Media

TV Documentaries

Highway (BBC: 1991)

An episode of the BBC religious programme, which involved two former members of *The Goon Show* – Harry Secombe and Michael Bentine – travelling on the RH&DR from New Romney to Dungeness (it is revealed in the programme that Bentine had travelled on the inaugural service from New Romney to Hythe in 1927).

Country Ways (ITV Meridian: 1998)

Episode of the gentle documentary series celebrating living in the country. This considered the lives of those people living at Dungeness and heavily featured Doris Tart (then aged 77).

Up Your Street (Channel 4: 2005)

This programme featured two of the Dungeness carriage conversions (Jesmond and At Last).

Homes by the Sea (Channel 4: 2014; series 1, episode 5)

Charlie Luxton visits a number of properties along the coast, which include two contrasting Dungeness buildings: Dunrunnin' and The Pobble House.

Holiday of a Lifetime (BBC: 2014; series 1, episode 15)

Episode featuring comedian Bill Oddie, who recreated a holiday of his youth. Starting at New Romney, he takes the RH&DR to Dungeness and revisits the bird observatory.

Grand Designs (Channel 4: 2015; Series 1, Episode 4)

This episode included views of a number of the Dungeness railway carriage conversions, and showcases The Pobble House (a House of the Year finalist). It rather annoyingly keeps alive the myth that Dungeness is a desert.

Walks with My Dog (Channel 4: 2017; series 1, episode 5)

Part of a series involving different celebrities, this episode featured Ben Fogle and his dog, Storm, walking the beach. It shows a number of classic Dungeness scenes and features the 1904 lighthouse.

Coast (BBC: various episodes)

This series featured various aspects of local history, which include Dungeness and the Lydd-on-Sea station area.

Ugly House to Lovely House (2019)

Episode of the Channel 4 show, which featured The Shingle House (as an example of what can be achieved, rather than showcasing its ugliness!).

TV entertainment

Doctor Who (BBC: 1971; season 8, episode 3)

Back in the sci-fi archives, this episode (*A Vampire From Space*) was part of a mini-serial, *The Claws of Axon*. The plot centres on the sucking dry of the energies of the earth – which include those of the power station! It has Jon Pertwee as the Doctor and Katy Manning as his assistant, and features shots of the power station as well as the beach. Filming took a week, one day of which was spent in the power station, and required the building of a monster ("Axon") on the beach. The army assisted with the filming and also provided a few acting "extras".

The Inspector Lynley Mysteries (BBC: 2006; series 5 episode 1)

Still regularly re-run on satellite channels, much of this episode (entitled *Natural Causes*) was filmed at Dungeness. It heavily features the RH&DR, Garden Cottage (where the fictional victim lives) and Pearl Cottage, at the time that the Smokery was operational. The finale takes place at the top of the 1904 lighthouse.

Eastenders (BBC: March 2007)

This was a "special" episode of the BBC1 soap, which opens with two characters standing on Dungeness beach. One alleges that he's been dumped there on a stag night, whilst the other claims to be waiting for a ferry. They adjourn to the Britannia pub, where they are also filmed playing pool.

The Poison Tree (ITV: 2012)

ITV two-part prime-time mini-series based on the psychological thriller of the same name by Erin Kelly. It stars Matthew Goode and MyAnna Buring as a couple who try to escape their past by moving to the Kent coast. Dungeness forms a major backdrop and many of the significant scenes were shot here.

Parades End (BBC: 2012)

Drama series based on novels by Ford Madox Ford. A number of Romney Marsh locations are featured, including Dungeness.

Philip K. Dick's Electric Dreams (Channel 4 and Sony Pictures: 2017; episode 4)

Filming of this episode (*Crazy Diamond*) of the science fiction anthology involved two Kent locations – the Cheyne Court windfarm and Dungeness. The Dungeness estate is used as background for a number of shots and The Pilot Inn also features.

Sick of It (Sky 2018; Episode 3)

An episode of the British comedy-drama television series starring Karl Pilkington as his namesake. In this episode, he tries to escape his domestic troubles by taking a holiday "in the middle of nowhere" – which just happens to be Dungeness! There is some good atmospheric footage of the fishing beach and scenes shot in both a fisherman's cottage and the light railway café (which has been fitted out with luxury furnishings for the purposes of filming).

Back to Life (BBC1/3 2019)

Some key scenes of this comedy drama (mainly set in Hythe) were shot at Dungeness. Both lighthouses and general footage are shown, and the Britannia pub features.

Peter Andre: My Life on the Beach (ITV2 2019)

Dungeness formed the backdrop for trailers for the "fly on the wall" reality series following the life of the Australian singer and TV personality.

Other TV programmes

Although full details are not to hand, the BBC have filmed sequences at Dungeness with Jeremy Clarkson for *Top Gear* episodes and with Jools Holland. Scenes from an episode of the BBC 1997 sitcom *Citizen Smith* and the ITV comedy drama *Minder* have allegedly also used Dungeness as a backdrop (but it has not been possible to confirm this). Channel 4 has also regularly broadcast idents shot on Dungeness beach.

Music/music videos

Freedom (2012) – Nicky Minaj

Nicki Minaj's video was shot extensively on Dungeness Beach and at the Greatstone sound mirrors. Minaj refused to walk on the shingle and insisted on a rickshaw bicycle to transport her. This took only eight men to push her over the soft terrain, so there was no risk of her being accused of being a diva!

Invaders Must Die (2009) – The Prodigy

Video features the old lighthouse (and also the acoustic mirrors at Greatstone).

Nanny Goat Island

High (1997) – The Lighthouse Family

From the album *Postcards from Heaven*, this video uses several locations and footage that includes scenes of Dungeness beach, pylons, fisherman's homes and the RH&DR line/level crossing.

Same Old Brand New You (2001) – A1

The boy band shot their video at Dungeness, with props apparently designed to make it appear more like the American west. More significant was the damage caused during filming, which led to court action being taken by English Nature.

Album covers

So much for the City – The Thrills (2003).

Aled – Aled Jones (2002).

A Collection of Great Dance Songs (1981) – Pink Floyd (cover shows Garden Cottage).

Bass Communion 2 (1999) – Bass Communion (cover shows the "T" fishing mark aid on Dungeness Beach).

Bass Communion 3 (2001) – Bass Communion (cover shows the old Marconi radio shed).

Keep calm and carry on (2009) – Stereophonics.

Individual songs/tracks

I'm Ebola (2010) – The Stripper Project (a Hastings band). The track from their album *Brilliant Life* mentions the nuclear power station ("I'm like a three-handed child in the shadow of Dungeness . . . where we can grow our extra toes"!).

Dungeness (2003) – Athlete (from their album *Vehicles and Animals*). Track includes the lyrics: "Go to Dungeness. Let's go to Dungeness".

Devil in Dungeness (2018) – Trembling Bells (a psych-folk band) from their album *Dungeness*.

Powerstation (2006) – November Coming Fire (a Kent punk band). Track from the album *Dungeness* which incorporates a recording of waves on the beach.

Lighthouse Keeper (2016) – Sam Duckworth (a musician who performs as "Get Cape. Wear Cape. Fly."). This track specifically mentions the Dungeness light.

Other Media exposure

Dungeness has additionally hosted photoshoots by supermodel Claudia Schiffer; and been used (in 2012) for testing the Olympic torch. The village has, too, featured in numerous radio broadcasts – notably on Radio 4. These have included episodes of *Excess Baggage* (presented live from The Pilot Inn by Sandi Tosvig [2004]); *Shingle Street* (a sound portrait of Dungeness [2010]); and *Wireless Nights* (featuring a night walk with Jarvis Cocker [2018]). The Radio 3 programme *Between the Ears* (*The Plot for Karl Marx* [2017]) featured the Dungeness Snack Shack.

In 20th century literature, Dungeness rates a number of mentions in Russell Thorndike's *Doctor Syn* saga, as well as within Malcolm Saville's *Lone Pine Mystery* series for teenagers. Of these books, *The Elusive Grasshopper* (published 1951) – is particularly notable, featuring both the old school and the RH&DR station. A 1964 novel by Ronald Johnston (*Disaster at Dungeness*) features attempts to rescue a vessel off the local coast. More recently, there has been a spate of books set in or featuring Dungeness. Novels by local authors include *The Homing Instinct* (Andrew Benedict [2012]) and a trilogy by Emma Batten (*Secrets of the Shingle* [2016]; *Stranger on the Point* [2018]; and *The Artist's Gift* [2019]). The 2017 novel, *A Dreadful Trade*, by CJ Bateman, is set largely in Dungeness (although re-named Shoreness; and its two pubs appear as the Lighthouse and the Lucky Fisherman), whilst the internationally-acclaimed journalist and author William Shaw sets his DS Alexandra Cupidi novels here (the officer owning a property in the village). These to date comprise *The Birdwatcher* (2016);[1] *Salt Lane* (2018); and *Deadland* (2019). Finally, Dungeness provides a key plot device in the 2016 TV comedy spin-off novel *Alan Partridge: Nomad*.

---

1. Renowned historical novelist CJ Sansom has praised this work for its "superb description of a haunting, blighted landscape"!

The New Playground of Kent

Greatstone and Littlestone Then and Now

By Keith Swallow

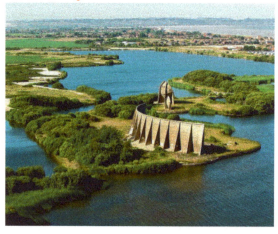

Many are familiar with Dungeness, but few are as aware of the charms of its neighbouring coastal villages. At the turn of the twentieth century, anyone who was anyone was a member of Littlestone Golf Club. Many, including serving and former Prime Ministers, members of the judiciary and even a Hollywood starlet, bought second homes here just to play the course.

In contrast, Greatstone – much of which was still under the sea in the 19th century – was marketed as the New Playground of Kent in the 1930s. Both these villages were in the invasion front line in World War II; and Greatstone was at the forefront of pioneering work that predated the invention of radar, also playing a pivotal role in the remarkable Pipe Line Under the Ocean (PLUTO) project. Whilst a glittering future was mapped out – plans included a pier at Littlestone – the area did not take off in the way envisaged; although it was not the quiet backwater that one of the Great Train Robbers had hoped when he tried unsuccessfully to find anonymity here. This book – which also covers the villages of Lade and Lydd-on-Sea – traces the history of this unique part of Romney Marsh and the individuals who have shaped its developmen

ISBN: 978-0-9933203-6-1
Price: £15 from any good bookshop
(or see www.edgertonpublishing.co.uk)

Much Drinking in the Marsh

A History of the Pubs and Breweries of Romney Marsh

By Keith Swallow

In this country, there are two complementary institutions that have been fundamental to the development of communities: the church and the pub. There has been much written – rightly – of the magnificence of Romney Marsh's churches, but less on its pubs. Yet, down the years, the Marsh has been served by some wonderful licensed establishments. Some of these have inevitably and unfortunately gone to the wall, although there are many fine examples still to be found. This book explores the history of the area's hostelries and breweries and seeks to address some of this imbalance. Within it you will find dark deeds, ghosts, eccentric landlords and more.

ISBN: 978-0-9933203-1-6
Price: £15 from any good bookshop
(or see www.edgertonpublishing.co.uk)

Also from
Edgerton Publishing Services

Pett in Sussex, by John Taylor, 2004, ISBN 978-0-9548390-0-0 (0-9548390-0-5) Price £15.00 – A history of the village.

A Changing Shore, An Illustrated Account of Winchelsea Beach, by Michael and Ruth Saville, 2006, ISBN 978-0-9548390-2-4, Price £12.00 – A history of this seaside community, covering also the Mary Stanford lifeboat disaster, Smeaton's Harbour and the Rye Harbour Nature Reserve.

A Survivor's Story, Prisoner of War to Parish Priest, by John Read, 2007, ISBN 978-0-9548390-3-1, Price £10.00 – Prisoner of the Japanese on the infamous Burma Railway and subsequently Rector of Pett, John Read tells his story with a remarkable lack of bitterness.

A Destiny Defined, Dante Gabriel Rossetti and Elizabeth Siddal in Hastings, by Jenny Ridd, 2008, ISBN 978-9548390-4-8, Price £10.00 – The story of the poet/painter and his muse during their happy days in Hastings, where they were married. The book goes on to consider the later, less happy, times.

My Early Years Down Under, by John (Jack) Edge, 2011 (revised edition), ISBN 978-0-9548390-8-6, Price £12.50 – An autobiographical account of an English migrant trying to find work in Western Australia at the beginning of the Great Depression, 1929–1930.

The Book of Syn: Russell Thorndike, Dr Syn and the Romney Marsh, by Keith Swallow, 2013, ISBN 978-0-9548390-9-3, Price £16.00 – The Dr Syn saga and its manifestations; separating fact from fiction.

The Jewish Ghost – Being German: A Search for Meaning, by Louise Illig-Mooncie, 2013, ISBN 978-0-9548390-6-2, Price £9.99 – One woman's search for meaning in post-war, post-Holocaust Germany.

Thiose were 'Dee Days', by Dee-Day White, 2015, ISBN 978-0-9933203-5-4, Price £10.00 – Growing up in the fishing community of Hastings Old Town.

The Viking Farm, by Unn Pedersen, 2016. ISBN 978-82-05-49695-8. Price £15.00 – Stories based on archaeology. A girl from the town visits her cousin on the farm.

The Viking Town, by Unn Pedersen, 2016. ISBN 978-82-05-49696-5. Price £15.00 – Stories based on archaeology. A boy from the farm visits his cousin in the town.

The Fallen of Pett, by David Breakell and Martin King, 2019. ISBN 978-0-9933203-2-3, Price £12.00. A historical memoir of the War Memorial at Pett in East Sussex and of the men it honours.

Boxed Off and Shipshape: a tale or two from a Sussex seafarer, by Cliff Arkley, 2021, ISBN 978-0-9933203-7-8, Price £19.99. Life in the merchant navy and the off-shore oil industry over the last fifty years, as told by the Rye-based author.

**Available from any good bookshop
(or see www.edgertonpublishing.co.uk)**